Meetings with My Master

Also by the Author

For Universal Minds
Teach Me to Fly
Head in the Stars, Feet on the Ground

Meetings with my Master

A Woman's Experience

by Nancy "Niiti" Gannon

InnerWorld Publications
San Germán, Puerto Rico
www.innerworldpublications.com

Copyright © 2017 by Nancy Gannon

All rights reserved under International and Pan-American Copyright Conventions. Published in the United States by InnerWorld Publications, PO Box 1613, San Germán, Puerto Rico, 00683.

Library of Congress Control Number: 2017917456

Cover Design: Devashish Donald Acosta

No part of this book may be reproduced or transmitted in any form or by any means, electronic or mechanical, including photocopying, recording, or by any information storage or retrieval system, without permission in writing from the publisher, except for the inclusion of brief quotations in a review.

ISBN: 9781881717607

For Baba

Contents

Introduction	1
1 My Life Changing Event In 1972	2
2 My Initiation	5
3 I Meet Dada Birendra Lal, a Family Acharya	7
4 Guru and Transformation	11
5 My First Trip to India	13
6 Meeting Dada Adveshananda	19
7 Experience with Dada Cidananda	27
8 Didi Ananda Bharati Teaches about Discipleship	29
9 Didi Asitiima, a Sweet Flame	34
10 First Meeting with the Master	38
11 Baba Visits Patna	43
12 Personal Contact with the Master	47
13 The Master Visits Bangkok	53
14 The Master Seizes My Acharyaship	63

15 The Master Gives Dharma Samikśa	69
16 Field Experience with the Master	78
17 Memorable 1980s	82
18 Neo-Humanism and Songs of the New Dawn	89
19 His New Garden Program	93
20 Discipline Experiences While Reporting	96
21 Flooded Quarters	102
22 I Become an Avadhutika	104
23 In Malaysia	110
24 Return to Manila	114
25 Australian Life	119
26 Guam Posting	123
27 Deep Sorrow	130
28 Taipei Life	137
29 Japan Days and the Return to the USA	140
Epilog	143
Postscript	144

Introduction

*A*s a young American woman I was fortunate to meet and become Shrii Shrii Anandamurti's disciple. At my first meeting with Him in 1979, He charged me with keeping His memory alive. He said, "Has the darshan been translated into English? It should be. It must be. It should be!" This book is my attempt to fulfill His request to me. It encompasses various darshans I had with the master. "Darshan" is a Sanskrit term that refers to a devotee being in the presence of her guru. At such meetings the disciple is blessed with glimpses of the Ultimate Truth by observing the spiritual nature of the guru.

1
My Life Changing Event In 1972

AMERICAN TEENS IN the 1970s witnessed the feminist movement, the hippie movement, Anti-Vietnam War demonstrations, and racial protests. I was nineteen years old in 1972 and inspired by these movements. They made me restless for change. I decided to stop attending Illinois State University while in my second year and to travel to Missoula, Montana. My older sister, Melody, lived there and I hoped by my visit to gain new direction in my life.

My sister and I were close siblings, a year apart. We complimented each other. Melody was taller, larger-boned, and blond, while I was shorter, smaller boned, and a brunette. She was poised and I was precocious. Throughout our childhood, I admired Melody and loved her company. Naturally, I believed she could aid my search for the meaning of life.

Unsure of how to help her younger sister, Melody took me on nature outings in Missoula, which is located along the Clark Fork River and meets five mountain ranges. In and around Missoula are thousands of acres of parkland and open, spacious conservation land. Melody and I explored the lush natural sights of these parks. Our experience was magnified by the summer meteor showers. On those nights shooting stars streaked across the clear, dark skies every few minutes. The stars looked like layers upon layers of brilliant celestial orbs. We could see deep into the Milky Way.

Besides the abundance of nature's beauty, Missoula is a university town and many activities center around university life. One evening Melody suggested we go to a lecture on meditation at the university. The talk would be given by followers of an international meditation, yoga, and service organization called "Ananda Marga," which means "Path of Bliss." The followers called themselves "Margiis."

Attending this introductory lecture changed my life. I was introduced to meditation and learned about the living master, Shrii Shrii Anandamurti, whose name means "the embodiment of bliss." His devotees more often referred to Him as "Baba," which means "Father" or "Beloved." The day after the lecture, I went alone to Ananda Marga's meditation center. The Margii residents there explained more of their spiritual practices and invited me to attend weekly meditations. I liked that they referred to each other as "brothers and sisters," and how they treated each other with warmth and respect. Before I left they gave me a handout which detailed crucial aspects of the Ananda Marga lifestyle.

Back at my sister's home, I studied the handout. It explained about adherence to ten moral principles. The handout also included a simple meditation process, three basic yoga postures, and information on a sentient vegetarian diet. I started these daily practices and found them challenging and dynamic. My new discipline set a course for positive, concrete change, like a map for life's stormy seas. Meditation, especially, stood out as the crown jewel in this treasure box of spiritual disciplines. I sensed that meditation, although being more elusive, was exactly what I needed.

When I began meditation, I sat upright with a straight spine to allow the nerve currents inside my spinal cord more freedom to flow. I placed my hands on my lap and sat on the floor with crossed legs. I closed my eyes, calmed my breath, and concentrated on repeating the universal mantra, *Baba Nam Kevalam*, which meant "Divine Consciousness is all there is."

I diligently incorporated these practices into my daily life, almost like a drowning person holding onto a life raft. Before visiting Montana I had thought mostly in terms of social change. Now I believed changing myself was as important, and I had learned a mystical means for it. Through meditation, I could attain a divine connection that before I read only about in books. Moreover, the guru, the creator of this meditation, lived in India and I might be able to meet Him. Maybe I could even participate in witnessing Him make history. However, I learned from the Margiis that Baba was in jail on false conspiracy charges. They said the Indian government was concerned over Ananda Marga's rapid expansion and their beliefs, which included anti-communist and anti-capitalist movements. His imprisonment was intended to weaken Ananda Marga. Instead, it strengthened the members' resolve. They made more effort to internationally grow its membership. At the time when I first met Ananda Marga there were many Ananda Marga meditation units existing throughout the US.

2
My Initiation

I OBSERVED THAT BOTH the guru and His followers were risking much for their beliefs. When I learned of the imprisonment of the guru, I respected Him more. I began to hope for Baba's release from jail. My meditative practices and moral efforts intensified, and my life felt like it was on track.

Secretly, I yearned to advance in meditation. The members told me any interested person could be initiated into a series of higher lessons from an acharya. There were no monetary fees for these lessons. A person needed only to demonstrate by her discipline the sincerity to learn. The Margiis in Missoula told me that an acharya named Dada Yatiishvarananda would soon visit to help interested persons learn a personal mantra. Anxious for further development, I awaited eagerly the acharya's arrival.

When I met Dada Yatiishvarananda he looked extraordinary, tall and lean, with a bright orange tunic, matching lungi (sarong), and turban. Dada had a long, black beard that reached down his chest, black-rimmed glasses, and a very pointed nose. His dark brown eyes scanned everyone quickly, seemingly to determine what he needed to do and why.

During my personal session with Dada Yatiishvarananda, we sat across from one another on our own meditation seats. He explained the initiation process and taught me my personal mantra. Later he reminded me to follow morality and to meditate twice a day.

A couple weeks later, in the autumn of 1972, I bid my sister and new Margii acquaintances goodbye and returned home to the Chicago area where my parents resided. Back at home, the new spiritual practices I had learned brightened my disposition. My life became more positive, making a good impression on my parents, convincing them that Ananda Marga's influence was beneficial. In fact, we meditated together a few times.

3
I Meet Dada Birendra Lal, a Family Acharya

While living at home I began working to earn enough to go back to college. I made it a habit to ride the train once a week to Chicago and attend a weekly group meditation there. The group meditations were held at the residence of a local family acharya, Dada Birendra Lal.

Usually, most Ananda Marga meditation teachers outside of India were monastic teachers who focused their time wholly on the mission. But historically the first acharyas of Ananda Marga were married householders. They were called "family acharyas." After the guru created the monastic system, fewer family acharyas were created. In Chicago, Dada Lal held the distinction of being one of the original family acharyas made before the monastic system began. These early family acharyas were personally chosen and taught by Baba.

Our meditation group consisted of ten to twenty people who sat on a carpeted floor in Dada's living room. Dada Lal was a lean, short-figured man who wore black trousers and a white office shirt. Usually, he would arrive just before our meditation time from his job as an engineer. In my experience, Dada Lal maintained at most times a calm and modest demeanor.

Each week Dada Lal led us in meditation and, after it, gave an inspirational talk. At the end of the evening, Dada's wife, wearing a traditional sari, would enter the room and greet us with "Namaskar," which meant, "I pay you my respect with all the divine charms of mind and all the love and cordiality of my heart." Then she offered us cookies. Their hospitality helped us feel like members of an extended family.

During our weekly meditations with Dada Lal some unusual phenomena occurred. I was still new in my spiritual efforts, yet I could see a white haze form above the group. It descended when we began chanting and disappeared after Dada Lal finished his spiritual address. Weekly meditations felt like the group was being transported to a more serene state that ended when Dada Lal completed his talk.

Many of the Margiis attending group meditation regularly had dreams of the guru. At this time I had my first Baba dream. In my dream, I joined a big gathering of Margiis. There was a group of women who took me aside and removed my hair adornments and jewelry. While doing this, they explained I did not need them anymore. Next, Baba arrived and a disciple requested Him that our group be allowed to carry Him down a flight of stairs. The group went to carry Baba, and I reached out to lift one of His feet. Upon touching His foot, a white light flooded my eyes as if a person had entered my dark bedroom and pulled open the window shades to let in the morning sun. Startled by the bright light, I opened my eyes to check the room. It was still dark; the shades were drawn. Closing my eyes again, I pondered the meaning of the dream and the feelings of well-being that it had aroused.

After that dream, I aspired to be a better person. Through the generous interactions with Dada Lal, and through Baba dreams, I understood that unconditional love touches a place deep inside. Without anyone asking, I offered to take over organizing the finances of the weekly meditation group. I also became involved in national Ananda Marga events. We organized a protest at the Indian Consulate in Chicago where we carried posters about Indira Gandhi's persecution of Baba. Later I joined other protests in Montreal, Canada, and Washington, D.C.

A critical incident at this juncture magnified my feelings for my guru. On February 12, 1973, under secret orders from the Central Bureau of Investigation (CBI), the prison physician, D. Rahamatulla, administered a lethal dose of barbiturates to Baba on the pretext that it was prescribed medicine. Baba went into convulsions and a coma but did not die. Upon regaining consciousness He filed a complaint against the prison doctor. Obtaining no results from His complaint, on April 1, 1973, Baba refused to take any more food supplied by the prison. Because the prison authorities denied food cooked outside the prison to be given him, Baba began His historic fast.

At the start of His fast, the Central Bureau of Investigation (CBI) threatened to force-feed Baba. Three months later, He began to daily take a watery yogurt drink comprised of three parts water and one part yogurt. It had little substance but stopped the CBI from force-feeding Him. His only source of food were these two cups of watery yogurt broth per day. His miraculous fast continued for the next five years, four months, and two days until His release from prison. He was fifty-two years old when He began His fast and fifty-eight when it ended.

Motivated by the suffering and endangerment of Baba, Margiis increased their protests around the world. When I heard of His poisoning and His miraculous fasting, I felt a growing awareness of Him and more anguish for His predicament. There was a greater urgency to help Baba. I became even more active in protests and His social service work. The more I did, the better my spiritual discipline and meditation became. In this way, two years quickly passed, and Dada Lal initiated me into the various meditation lessons of Ananda Marga.

Before learning the last lesson, there needs to be a strong relationship between the initiate and the guru. In the last instruction, called "dhyana," the disciple establishes an intense connection with their guru during meditation. In Sanskrit an ancient adage says:

Dhyan mulam gururmurti
Puja mulam gurur padam'
Mantra mulam guru vakyam
Moks'a mulam guru krpa

(The root of dhyana is the form of the guru. The root of surrender is the guru's feet. The root of mantra is the word of the guru. The root of salvation is guru's grace.)

Practicing dhyana and the other lessons clarify for the meditator that self-realization is possible with effort and the guru's help. One time I asked Dada Lal about it. He explained, "When you meditate, focus your mind into a single point, become one with that point, and bathe in divine radiance."

Regularly I was increasingly pointing my mind toward my guru.

4
Guru and Transformation

*A*LTHOUGH I WOULD wait to meet Baba in person, the system of transformation He started was having an effect. The more engrossed I became in meditation and in Ananda Marga activities, the more I changed. I was growing happier and my heart was beginning to love this mysterious guru, Baba.

I noticed that during meditations, especially group meditations, a blissful intoxicating feeling often came. In ways it was similar to a strong glass of wine: the world mellowed and filled with well-being. The difference was the "high" from meditation left a crystalline clarity that could be called upon if needed. As in the ancient writings of the *Rubaiyat of Omar Khayyam*, the drinking cup was meditation and intoxication was ecstasy.

Quatrain 37

Ah, fill the Cup: - what boots it to repeat
How Time is slipping underneath our Feet:
Unborn TO-MORROW, and dead YESTERDAY,
Why fret about them if TO-DAY be sweet![1]

Since learning meditation I had listened to many interesting stories about Baba. I appreciated that He could communicate in the various languages of His disciples. He had demonstrated that He spoke over a hundred languages. Many stories told about how

---

1   Fitzgerald, E., *The Rubaiyat Of Omar Khayyam, the Astronomer-Poet of Persia*, (London, B. Quaritch, 1st ed., 1859).

He used intuitive powers to strengthen His disciples' faith and broaden their outlook. People who had attended a spiritual gathering with Baba remarked that sometimes Baba seemed to look only at them and at other times Baba seemed to look at everyone else but them. In this manner, they knew they were being singled out by their master.

Baba once said that before He began a spiritual discourse He would look over the heads of His attending disciples and ascertain the questions in their hearts. Then, when He spoke, He would answer each one. That is why reading His discourses answers many of a disciple's questions.

I do not know how, but Baba drew me closer. My yearning for Him grew, as well as my concern for His well-being in prison. History would record that throughout most of the 1970s Baba sacrificed so much through His poisoning, fasting, and jail treatment. To encourage His disciples during this difficult period, Baba predicted that in the future, PROUT, a moral and just universal government, would be established. Those future inhabitants, after Prout's establishment, would enjoy a better world but they would wonder what was life like with Baba.

5
My First Trip to India

*I*N 1974, WHEN I was twenty-one, my love for Baba and His mission reached such a crescendo that I chose to dedicate my life to His service. I said a tearful goodbye to my family and left the United States for India, where I would train to become an acharya.

When the plane arrived at Kolkata's hot and dusty Dum Dum International Airport, I felt that I had alighted from a time machine and landed in the past. India was a stark contrast to middle-class American suburbia, where people owned cars and washing machines. In awe and respect for Baba's homeland, I bent and touched the dust of the Kolkata tarmac.

Walking out of the airport terminal, I noticed men and women squatting and chewing betel nuts. They occasionally spat on the ground next to them, leaving large red stains on the dirt. I noticed their teeth and tongues had the same red stains. Carefully I walked around them and the red stains. Later some Indian Margiis said that Baba discouraged the use of betel nut since it made people slightly intoxicated.

To reach the Ananda Marga headquarters, I hired an old-looking taxi cab. Sitting inside the cab, I felt the heat and dust of Kolkata streets, which teemed with life. Cows roamed freely on the streets. Small herds of goats and water buffalo grazed along the roadsides. Old, refurbished cars from the forties and fifties deftly maneuvered the road, their drivers honking and waving their arms out of the car window, instead of using turn signals.

Women walked the dirt paths next to the road in colorful cotton saris of maroons, reds, blues, and greens, while they carried bundles atop their heads. I noticed wealthier ladies dressed in nylon and silk saris, their arms jingling with a variety of gold bangles.

The scent of sweet incense hung in the warm air and intertwined with the aroma of pungent spiced foods and smoke from cow dung stoves. In some areas, there were sulfuric smells of garbage piled along the road. I observed that poor people would sort through the piles and then leave the rest for the goats to chew on.

My first night was spent at Ananda Marga's central office, located in the Jodhpur Park area. The next morning, along with another trainee, I boarded a crowded, steam-driven overnight train to Varanasi. We traveled together many miles into the mysterious depths of central India, finally arriving at our destination.

Varanasi is one of the oldest and holiest cities in the world. It existed before the founding of most of the world's major religions. According to legend, Varanasi was founded by Shiva seven thousand years ago. Around four thousand years later the Pandavas, heroes of the Mahabharat, visited there to atone for their sins. Around 460 BCE Gautama Buddha gave his first sermon at Sarnath, which is near Varanasi. Throughout the centuries many saints, poets, writers, and musicians lived there.

At the train station, we hired a pulled rickshaw to take us to the training center. The didis' training center was formerly the dadas' center until they built one. It was situated in the second story of a large family home. It had its own entrance, a veranda, a small visitors' room, two bedrooms, and one large room used for storage and cooking.

There were ten women trainees from different nations such as India, Philippines, Australia, United States, and Germany. All the trainees slept on the floor atop grass mats. On hot nights they slept outside on the veranda. If a trainee was sick, she was given a wooden platform bed to sleep on.

The only latrine for the trainees was located on the veranda outside. Water had to be carried up each day from the well located in the family's yard. Every able-bodied trainee helped fetch water from it for cleaning and drinking. Each morning the trainees bathed and washed their saris against the rocks alongside the well.

Most of the meals were similar, consisting of rice, chapattis, and vegetables, which were prepared by sitting on the floor in front of a single, sawdust-fueled stove. Each dish was cooked, one-by-one, atop that single burner. Every healthy trainee had a cooking duty. Most trainees dreaded the sawdust fueled stove. It took significant time to pack down the sawdust in its center chamber. It was crucial that it be packed well; otherwise, the sawdust would cave in while cooking.

While I was in training there were very few visitors. Each day we met with the trainer dada who would visit in the afternoon. He taught in the visitors' room an hour-long class to each group of trainees. We studied Oxford English, Sanskrit, and Bengali. We read social philosophy, memorized Sanskrit aphorisms, pondered Eastern cosmology, and memorized conduct rules. We learned the science of meditation and did long hours of practice, both by ourselves and collectively. Other than classes and chores, we visited with each other and studied. Our training environment was stark but the subtle nature of our study and the friendships we formed made us feel fortunate to be there. I and my classmates often wondered if we would be able to exemplify the high standards of acharyaship.

Once during our training, we had a special visitor. Her name was Avadhutika Ananda Karuna Acharya. She was the first woman avadhutika I ever met, and historically she was the third avadhutika created by Baba. She appeared to be in her late twenties and wore an orange sari and an orange long-sleeved tunic that reached her knees. On her head was a traditional nun's orange veil that draped over her shoulders and down the back and front to her waist. To inspire us, Didi Ananda Karuna told how she became a nun:

"When I arrived at the didis' quarters to attend acharya training, at first the other two didis did not believe I was qualified. I was very young and from a rural background. They started to arrange for my return train ticket back home. Before they could enact their plans, Baba interceded and sent a message to Didi Ananda Bharati. He stated that I should be allowed to attend acharya training. He said that I had a trishul-shaped birthmark on my leg, although I do not know how Baba knew this. He said I was meant to be an avadhutika."

The trishula, which resembles Neptune's trident, dates back to the first yoga master, Shiva, seven thousand years ago. Each point of the trident symbolizes one of the three psychic channels in the spine — *susumna*, *ida*, and *pimgala*. It is part of the avadhutika's full dress and apparatus. As Didi Ananda Karuna related this experience to us in the training center, she showed us her birthmark. We were very impressed. Through her inspirational story, encouragement, and personal example we grew stronger in our desire and more clear about what we aspired to be.

After Didi left, I studied hard for my tests. A few months later I sat for examinations with Dada Desaratha, the examiner. He was one of the first acharyas that Baba created, and he had an aura of a person who had great intuitive depth. For the first part of the exam, he asked me to write some English sentences that he dictated. Because I was a native English speaker, I felt cocky that I easily knew this part of the exam. However, Dada Desaratha told me some of my answers were not completely correct. He reminded me that I was being tested on Oxford English, not American English. After this, I became humble and focused and thus did well enough to pass the exam.

My training had finished in seven months. Often acharya training averaged one to two years. I succeeded so quickly, in part, because in the United States I had attended three months of Ananda Marga's Local Full Timer training. During it, I had memorized *Ananda Sutram* and conduct rules. Then, prior to leaving the United States, I memorized thirty Sanskrit *shlokas* (aphorisms).

Another reason for my shorter training I did not learn about until months later. The head dadas and didis at the central office knew the political climate was worsening toward Ananda Marga. Soon, they believed, there would be violence. Therefore they wanted the overseas trainees to quickly finish or to transfer to Nepal before it erupted. We trainees were not aware of what they thought or of the threat of violence against Ananda Marga.

The last part of my training took place in our central office in Kolkata. Upon arriving there, we attended additional classes and sat for another exam. I became an acharya in December 1974 and received a new name, Nandita. My official title was Acharya Nandita Brahmacarinii. The meaning of my name was "she who maintained a blissful mood." Didi Ananda Karuna helped me with my first uniform, which consisted of an orange tunic, an orange veil, and a white sari. This was our junior brahmacarinii dress. Didi Ananda Karuna also cut off my hair to the scalp.

During my last days of training, I met the head of the women's department, Didi Ananda Bharati, who was affectionately called "Auntie." She was the first woman to be made an avadhutika by Baba. Auntie was older in age and very intuitive, and I felt glad to meet her.

After training, a new didi would usually present herself to Baba before or after His field walk. Then she would offer Him a flower garland. Unfortunately, due to the circumstances of His incarceration, this did not occur. Hopefully, one day soon, I would meet Baba.

After becoming an acharya, I left quickly for my assignment in Australia. It was January of 1975. While in Australia I learned that on July 3, 1975 a nation-wide emergency was imposed by the Indian national government banning Ananda Marga. Many other organizations and groups across the country fell under this ban, and this historical period later became known as "The Emergency."

For twenty-one months, from June 25, 1975 until March 21, 1977, Prime Minister Indira Gandhi had a unilateral state of emergency declared across the country. The new order bestowed upon the prime minister the authority to rule by decree, allow her to suspend elections and curb civil liberties. Ananda Marga and other political opponents of Gandhi were jailed and the press censored. During The Emergency several atrocities occurred, including a forced mass-sterilization campaign spearheaded by Gandhi's son. This was the leading cause of Indira Gandhi's election loss in 1977, after she ended the state of emergency.

During The Emergency most acharyas were in jail or fled underground to avoid arrest. It became difficult to ensure Baba's welfare. Since His poisoning and fast, only a few had access to help Him. These were His personal assistant Dada Ramananda, and the new jail doctor who replaced Dr. Kalawar, the one Baba accused of poisoning Him. Secretly Dada Ramananda and the new jail doctor conspired and invented ways to maintain Baba's well-being and to keep communication between Baba and His workers open.

From His arrest until He was vindicated, Baba was denied bail and remained incarcerated. On November 29, 1976, He and four co-accused acharyas received a sentence of life imprisonment. They were convicted of conspiring to murder some Ananda Margii followers. Representatives of Amnesty International, the International Commission of Jurists, and the International League for Human Rights attended the court proceedings. A member of the Canadian Bar, Mr. Claude-Armand Sheppard, in a report commissioned by the International Commission of Jurists and the International League for Human Rights wrote: "Reading the Indian press and official comments about Ananda Marga, as well as listening to some of the witnesses called by the prosecution, one cannot avoid the conclusion that a governmental witch-hunt has been instituted against anyone associated with Ananda Marga."

6
Meeting Dada Adveshananda

*B*EFORE THE EMERGENCY, after only three months of living in Australia, my assignment was changed to Manila, Philippines. The transfer was exciting for me, as Baba had visited Manila twice and reported how devotional the Margiis were during His visit. Baba had named the Philippines "Maharlika," meaning "a small place that holds something great."

Within a week of my transfer, I flew to Manila. Upon disembarking from the plane, I was greeted by a small group of youthful members and one middle-aged avadhuta named Dada Adveshananda.

My first impression of Dada Adveshananda was that he looked less sharply dressed than other dadas. His orange turban was crooked, with a strand untied. His nose was pointed and had a break in it. He had long, well-oiled, black and gray hair. When he smiled I noticed a chipped front tooth. Plus he walked with crutches. Despite his odd appearance, I sensed that I stood in the presence of a seer. The electrical aura around him impelled me to bow and touch his feet, as is customary in India to an elder. At this gesture, he remarked to me, "Those who surrender their egos can truly learn."

When he said that, I had an epiphany that I could trust Dada Adveshananda as a mentor. Flashes of insight often are immediate and effortless, as was mine at that moment. After the introductions, our group sped away from the airport in one Margii's custom van, a vehicle popular in the Philippines called a "jeepney." On the way to the jagrti (yoga center), we loudly chanted Baba Nam Kevalam, "love is all there is."

The jagrti was an old Spanish residence that had its own gated compound. The women residents lived on the second floor while the men stayed on the main floor. Twelve to twenty volunteers at a time lived in the meditation center. It was located in Paco, a district of Manila, easily reached from most areas of the city and within walking distance of a vegetable market. On its street corner sat a bakery, which served wonderful fresh hot "pan de sol" bread that we ate regularly.

During the daytime I often accompanied Dada and the local full time volunteers, or LFTs, to lectures on meditation or to do social service. Occasionally in the evenings, a group of us would ride a Margii's jeepney to the local cemetery. There we would sit and meditate together. It was serene and eerily still. Once, Dada Adveshananda explained, "You should aspire to feel no fear here. Rather make yourself feel as safe in the graveyard as in your own bedroom; then you will become strong-minded and be at home everywhere."

During this period, wherever or whatever service we did, we usually did as a group, like a large loving family. These experiences gave me insight that I was a part of a blissful, universal family. Life with Dada Adveshananda was dramatic and colorful, full of songs, service, and public talks. "Keep them busy singing Baba Nam Kevalam, performing service, and their minds engaged in good thoughts," seemed his motto.

He often said, "Make yourself purer. Make your mind purer."

The primary area where we did service was Isla Putting Bato in Tundo, the largest and vilest slum in Manila. It was located next to a huge garbage dump by the main port of Manila. Tens of thousands of squatters lived in hovels atop rocks and stilts that jutted out of the black breakwater. Rotting wood planks made up pathways throughout the slum and if one looked down between the planks they would see the dirty sea water and sewage below. The stench of human waste and trash filled the air, and usually a cacophony of blaring radios intermingled with the sounds of children at play.

Isla Putting Bato had masses of children. Most of them sported bloated bellies from scurvy and their heads and bodies were covered with scabs. Because there were so many children, we limited our service to those aged two to five. In the afternoon when we arrived, a volunteer would tell nearby children to fetch their younger brothers and sisters and to bring an empty cup for milk. When fifty to a hundred children gathered, we began singing songs with the children. We taught them how to chant Baba Nam Kevalam. Afterward, we distributed to each child biscuits and milk that was heated in a big kettle.

On one such afternoon, a small group of adults approached us after our program with the children and asked for help. They brought us to a nearby open space that had been turned into a basketball court with a homemade basketball hoop. There on the sidelines of the court sat a child's small wooden coffin atop blocks of wood. Nearby children continued playing basketball next to it. We learned from the villagers that the coffin had been there for a few days, sitting in the hot sun. The parents could not raise enough money to bury it. Dada Adveshananda told the villagers that we would help. He told our driver to take us to the nearest shopping district. For three hours we walked, store to store, asking for donations for the burial of that child's coffin. After we raised enough, we returned to Isla Puting Batu and gave the money to the grateful family.

Regularly doing mass feeding programs with the children prepared me for another kind of service. On August 16, 1976, a 7.9 earthquake hit Mindanao Island and created a tsunami that devastated seven hundred kilometers of coastline. The estimated number of victims in this tragedy included five thousand dead, more than two thousand presumed dead, nine thousand five hundred injured and ninety-three thousand homeless. The worst hit area was Pagadian City, where the waves had reached higher than four meters.

Dada Adveshananda arranged for a small group of us to board a Philippine military plane to do service in Pagadian the day after the tragedy. We put cotton in our ears and sat on small metal seats while hanging onto straps in the non-insulated hull of an army plane. After disembarking we toured some of the affected areas where buildings were ruined and bodies were still not recovered. Most of the homeless survivors had gathered onto the highest ground of the city to camp in a park. We chose this site to do service. Since we had not come with many supplies or funds, we repeated the procedure we used in Isla Putting Batu. We gathered the children to sing; afterward, we distributed milk and cookies to them.

At first, I felt self-conscious about how little we had to offer to these homeless people. However, when we gathered the children to sing songs and chant Baba Nam Kevalam, I noticed it had a calming effect on the children. The adults, drew near to watch and relaxed. Hearing the children sing eased their shock and grief. I understood that there were many levels of service and that money alone could not uplift the victims. More importantly, I was gaining knowledge of the power of Baba Nam Kevalam. After a few days of participating in these kinds of activities, I returned by military plane to Manila. Dada Adveshananda and a few volunteers remained weeks longer.

Over time I became more accustomed to living in the Philippines and began to tour various islands. At that time, I was the only didi in the entire country, and I traveled extensively to initiate women in meditation and encourage them to do service. While traveling I observed Maharlika's beauty. Outside of Manila most of the islands were lush and green. The mountainous islands were canopied with tropical rainforests. There were abundant coconut, palm, and banana trees, and other tropical vegetation. Possibly, due to this rich landscape, people living in the provinces generally extended their generosity and hospitality to a degree that I had not experienced before. I would usually stay the night in a member's home, and upon leaving would be given a donation to help me in my work. Then I would go on to my next destination.

Although many Filipinos lived comfortably, they lived more simply than those in developed nations. Few had modern conveniences such as automobiles, washing machines, and gas ranges. I found this ironic since the Philippines were tremendously wealthy in natural resources. It held the second largest gold deposits in the world and was a top producer of copper. But the disparity between the very rich and the rest of the population was vast.

Occasionally while touring, I would meet up with Dada Adveshananda on some island and briefly enjoy his blissful inspiration. After a couple of years, though, he stopped touring and chose to stay in Manila. More male and female acharyas had arrived and he guided them, along with the local full time volunteers and the members. He kept us spiritually focused and reminded us that Baba was the inspiration behind our efforts.

Once at a large training seminar in Manila for acharyas and full timers, Dada Adveshananda made us aware in a dramatic way of the divine play of life. It began when a distinguished lay member, who was an executive in a large company, instructed the acharyas how to use management skills. The presentation was informative but it did not contain spiritual information. Dada Adveshananda arrived a little after it began and quickly assessed this. Toward the end of the seminar, our trainer had organized a demonstration to illustrate a chief point via two games, one of chance and one of skill. The game of chance involved spinning a bottle, whereby the contestant would succeed if the spinner stopped in the winning direction. In the game of skill, the contestant won by throwing balls into a basket. The trainer hoped to drive home that skill was superior to chance. He asked, "Which strategy should you rely on as you plan your Ananda Marga activities in daily life?"

By now Dada Adveshananda had experienced enough and would not remain quiet. He demanded to be the first participant to come up front, and he chose the game of chance over the game of skill. Lying down with his head propped up by his arm, he flicked the bottle to start it spinning. We all watched in amazement as the bottle kept going around and around. It continued to spin around and around, far beyond the normal period it should take. It came to a stop slowly and pointed toward the winning direction. Chaos broke out as we laughed loudly and said, "Dada Adveshananda, you used occult power."

The mood of the seminar had changed to one of an electrically charged spiritual drama. Dada told, "All is due to Baba. Devotion will always save you. Through His grace and through devotion one can obtain anything."

From the atmosphere of a seminar, we were again transformed into a blissful universal family at play in Baba's divine drama. Dada Adveshananda reminded us that Baba was with us when we sang, served, and meditated. We only needed to remember Him always.

Until he left Maharlika and returned to India, I remained in regular contact with Dada Adveshananda. One day he told me that soon he would be leaving. This occurred on the same day another senior dada named Dada Cidananda arrived. Dada Adveshananda introduced me and explained, "I did not want to leave Maharlika until someone very capable came. Now with Dada Cidananda's arrival, it is time for me to depart."

Dada Adveshananda explained that Dada Cidananda's duty would be to set up a wholetimer training center in Maharlika so desiring acharya candidates did not have to go to India for training. Baba had given this directive from prison. I was happy for this new development but was amazed by it. Over the past three years, Dada Adveshananda had often said that in the future acharya training would be available in Maharlika. I had thought he was just giving encouragement. But Dada Adveshananda had insisted, "Nothing is more important than devotion. If you have devotion, Baba will make it happen."

One last story of Dada Adveshananda occurred six years later when I no longer worked in Manila Sector. At that time I was near Suva, Fiji, visiting a family who had a rural farm on Mount Tomanivi. Another dada, newly arrived from India, was visiting that family, too. During a brief conversation with the new dada, we exchanged stories and spoke of whom we might know in common. He mentioned Dada Adveshananda and I grew excited and said, "I hold him in great esteem as one of the most inspiring dadas."

The new dada responded, "Then I am sorry to tell you that Dada Adveshananda is no more."

"No more? What do you mean, no more?" I asked.

"He died some months ago."

Tearing up I replied, "Dada is dead? How did he die?"

He explained, "Dada had been doing field work near Jamalpur, India. You know that is a special area since Baba spent His childhood there and the first members of Ananda Marga live in that area."

I replied that I knew.

"Dada Adveshananda appeared ill, so the local members arranged for him to visit the hospital. After a couple of days stay in the hospital he seemed better and the doctors discharged him. From the hospital, Dada Adveshananda went straight to the nearby Ananda Marga primary school for a visit. He went into a room that they reserved only for Baba to use whenever He visited the school. A young local full timer left Dada Adveshananda sitting alone in Baba's room while he went to fetch the dada a drink of water. When the volunteer returned, Dada had left his body. He died peacefully while sitting in Baba's room, his thoughts surely on Baba.

"I arrived in Jamalpur the day he died, as Baba had ordered me to go immediately to Jamalpur and replace Dada Adveshananda in his work. The Jamalpur Margiis and Dada Adveshananda did not know I was coming. Before entering the hospital, I learned that Dada Adveshananda had given away all his possessions. My arrival that day ensured he had a replacement for his work. Dada had left his body with every detail attended to.

"Some Filipino Margiis were so sad when they heard of Dada Adveshananda's death that they went to see Baba to ask Him why he died so soon. Baba told them that Dada Adveshananda had other work to do."

After hearing this story, I left to be alone and grieve Dada Adveshananda's passing. Later I took a walk; the sunset looked unusually splendid in shades of orange, green, and purple, as if in tribute to the passing of a dear devotee. I thought, Dada Adveshananda even managed to inform me of his death by having a dada who knew many details visit this mountain farm in Fiji. Just like Dada Adveshananda taught, "Devotion makes anything possible."

Dada Adveshananda

7
Experience with Dada Cidananda

*M*Y RELATIONSHIP WITH Dada Cidananda was different than my relationship with Dada Adveshananda. His posting as acharya trainer left him very busy, especially as he was establishing the wholetimer training center anew. He taught daily many young people and was rarely alone. Even though I had fewer direct interactions with Dada Cidananda, he set a great example. One of the main things I observed and took to heart happened during his initial spiritual talk, after a collective meditation in Paco, Manila. He said, "We have to love Baba more and more. We need to love Him so much that Baba can feel our love while He sits in India's jail or wherever He might be."

Listening to Dada Cidananda talk, I felt this love shine from him and believed Baba could perceive such strong devotion while He sat in India. Even now I think of it and try to love Baba like that so Baba can feel my yearning for Him wherever He may be.

One of my most exceptional intuitive experiences occurred during a visit to Dada Cidananda at the new training center. On that occasion, I was assisting some local Margii sisters in establishing a kindergarten in Digos, Davao Del Sur, a town close to Davao where the dadas training center was located. Fortunately, the nearness of Digos to Davao allowed me to make an overnight sojourn to the training center.

Usually, Dada Cidananda's habit was to visit the didis training center daily and give the trainees classes and supervise their service projects. Sometimes he stayed and led group meditation in the early evening. That evening there were about twenty people, mostly women trainees. A loud rain poured down and before we began meditation Dada Cidananda said, "Those who like the rain should remain at the finish of group meditation and continue meditation on their own."

I liked rain, so I stayed meditating when the group finished. I heard the rain beat on the corrugated iron that roofed the large hall. It sounded like a constant drumbeat. Then I heard marching music come from the left side of the roof. I wondered, "Who is playing this music so loud that I can hear it in this large hall?"

After finishing my meditation I still heard the marching music. Despite the rain, I searched for its source outside the building, but there was none. I could not find anyone playing music outside or inside. By this time I understood that no one had made that music. Rather it was celestial melodies that resounded. I went into my room and did yoga while listening to the band in the sky. Over time it changed from a march to a stringed sonata, then back to a march, and lastly a funeral dirge. Hearing the funeral hymn gave me an eerie, uncomfortable feeling and I wanted it to stop. I diverted my listening from the celestial music to listening to a woman in a nearby room playing guitar and chanting Baba Nam Kevalam. As I listened to her chanting, the celestial music faded and disappeared.

I did not speak to anyone of my mystical experience, primarily because it felt too profound to describe. The next morning when Dada Cidananda visited he asked me, "Did you like staying in the training center? Did you have a good experience here?"

I responded, "Yes, in fact, I did. I heard celestial music after group meditation."

He smiled and did not ask more. For the next couple of weeks, I occasionally heard wisps of celestial tunes again at odd times. These were often provoked by listening to a loud sound like a train or a machine hum. Over the years, I have come to believe that I heard my life story in a musical form that night in the rainstorm.

8
Didi Ananda Bharati Teaches about Discipleship

MANY WONDERFUL PEOPLE were drawn to my guru. Among these Avadhutika Ananda Bharati, or Auntie, stands out. As head of the Women's Welfare Department for over a decade, she influenced the direction that my discipleship took. With her words and manner, she helped me envision the life of a female disciple.

Auntie married in the arranged Indian style while young. She raised her children to adulthood and then organized their marriages. When her children were settled she renounced family life to participate more in spiritual pursuits. One major event from her early life Auntie described to me: "My elder sister was very pious. When she became ill and was dying, she called me to her and blessed me. This changed my life to a more spiritual direction."

For years Auntie was a devout disciple of another guru. After he died, she had a dream telling her that a saffron-clad monk would visit and initiate her into deeper spiritual practices. Shortly following her dream, an Ananda Marga acharya visited that area and taught her meditation. Then Auntie went to meet Baba.

When Baba met Auntie, He asked her to become His acharya and first avadhutika. Through Auntie, He developed the Women's Welfare Department (WWD), which she headed as long as she lived. When Auntie began her service to Baba she was mature in age. After a few years of touring, she stopped traveling. She became unable to even leave her bedroom. Most important planning meetings took place in her room. Her room was the hub of the didis' activities. A steady stream of junior and senior didis, dadas, and Margiis would visit her and share their accomplishments, woes, and funny stories. To all, Auntie had encouraging and wise words to share.

At one of our first meetings, she told me, "A disciple needs to develop much faith in the guru. When you do not understand something that Baba asks of you, have blind faith in Him."

She continued, "Do you not put such faith in the taxi driver that you hire when you go to Baba's quarters? Do you not have blind faith that the taxi driver will take you to your destination? When you get into the taxi, you do not know what will happen but you have faith that the driver will bring you safely to your destination. This same blind faith you should have with your guru, and he will take you to your divine destination."

Another time, while I was struggling as a new nun in the Philippines, she sent a letter to remind me how important it was to become an acharya. "A Margii should first ascertain if she can be a whole-time missionary worker," she wrote, "and only if she cannot be, then should she pursue marriage. Baba's need for acharyas is very great."

My favorite saying of hers was in response to a frustration that I shared with her. After I entrusted my difficulty to Auntie she explained, "Baba has infused so much red (the action principle) into Ananda Marga that nothing can stay the same way for long. Soon your difficulty will pass."

This I experienced again and again. There existed so much dynamism under Baba's guidance that the organization was perpetually in a whirlwind of activities. Every few months some worker in my field would be transferred and a new one arrive. Regularly I was sent to tour a new place to teach meditation and do service work. From jail, Baba would issue new targets for His workers to carry out. Life sped by and change was the only constant.

Whenever I traveled to India to report to the central office, I would first go to Auntie's room and touch her feet. Only then did

I feel I was home and belonged there. Often I visited Auntie and sat in her room while many important work of the didis' central office took place. Before I left to go back to my posting, I touched her feet again, hoping to show her my deep regard and to take her good will with me.

Over the years, I watched her grow increasingly ill and felt fortunate for every moment spent with her. Sometimes Auntie would point to her sick body and say, "I don't know why Baba won't give me permission and sign my tour program to let me go. He has added years to my life."

I believe Baba extended her life and did not let her die because we needed her so much. Auntie exemplified how a loving, intelligent, and spiritually mature didi acted. Next to my guru, she was the most formative person in my adult life.

Of all her teachings, I am particularly grateful for her guidance in Tantra. What is Tantra? Tantra was established in India seven thousand years ago by Shiva. Tantra is a comprehensive practice that covers every personal and social aspect of life. Literally translated, Tantra means "that which liberates the mind from dullness by expansion."

The goal is to expand oneself from a finite existence to an infinite one by penetrating the mystical link between the individual and the cosmos. In tantric practice, a person does not ignore the importance of daily life. Rather, every aspect of mundane life and of the phenomenal world is understood to be an expression of the Infinite. Therefore daily life can be transformed into a spiritual practice whether one is talking of health, philosophy, or meditation. All activities when properly executed become part of a concerted flow toward social and human emancipation.

Auntie explained to me that the traditional way for tantric pupils to study with the master was by the gurukul system. Historically, the disciples lived with their master and served him for years, absorbing every aspect of their guru's life, habits, and teachings. When the master felt a disciple was ready, he sent the disciple into the world, possibly never to see him again. The guru had carefully planted seeds that would grow and unfold throughout the disciple's life, living inside the disciple's dreams, memories, and thoughts.

Auntie implied that I should learn as much as I can about Baba and His teachings. In as many ways as possible I should integrate His life with mine. With her help, I grew stronger at linking my life with His. I began to view how Baba, similar to Shiva, had begun a movement to uplift the individual and society in essential ways. However, unlike the masters of yore, He had thousands of male and female disciples across the globe, which meant not every disciple could live with Him. Therefore He introduced various systems, especially the "Sixteen Points," to keep the link between the disciples and the guru. Through His representatives, the Sixteen Points, and dhyana meditation, Baba guided His disciples.

Auntie was very knowledgeable about Baba's daily schedule. He lived in such a systematic manner that His disciples could know His schedule and habits. His usual schedule went:

3:00 a. m. Wake
3:00 to 8:00: Spiritual practices, bath, drink lemon water, rest, and then spiritual practices again
8:00 to 10:00: Open door; His personal assistant gives Him His mail and he reads the newspapers
10:00 to 11:00: Garden walk and breakfast
11:00 to 12:00: Field walk
1:00 to 3:00: Office, listen to reporting, and bath
3:00: Lunch, walk one hundred steps, rest, receive a massage, and listen to reporting
7:30 to 9:00: Spiritual practice, bath, and dinner
9:00 to 10:00: Field walk
10:30 to 11:30: Listen to reporting, receive a massage, and meditation
12:00 to 3:00: Sleep

Often I saw Auntie look out the window to see Baba when He drove by during His daily outings. She routinely asked what Baba said or did that day to anyone who came from His quarters. I imitated Auntie and, when I was in the field, would calculate what time it was in India compared to my local time. Based on Baba's schedule I would guess what He might be doing at that moment. In this way, I infused my routine with Baba's. By this means I hoped to refine myself and make my life deeply entwined with His.

9
Didi Asitiima, a Sweet Flame

*B*ESIDES AUNTIE, THERE were other inspirational didis who influenced me. One more that I especially remember was a very young junior didi named Didi Asitiima, whom I knew for just a short time.

Didi Asitiima originally hailed from Switzerland and when we met she had just finished acharya training in Europe. Her first assignment was to work in Manila, and she came to relieve me of my duties so that I could start a new post called Sectorial Hari Pari Mandala Gosthi-Ladies (HPMGL). Baba had recently expanded the Women's Welfare Department and that was one of the new sections of our department. New didis were arriving to work in the Philippines to take on the new positions. My HPMGL assignment involved arranging activities for women to sing devotional songs and dance kiirtan, as well as other social service.

These new orders came directly from Baba, who was still suffering in jail. Neither Didi Asitiima or I had yet met Him, although we felt His presence and love in our daily life and knew we belonged to His universal family. When we were together we often talked about how we missed Baba and how wrong His imprisonment was. We were both twenty-six years old and enjoyed sharing our thoughts with each other. How very glad I am that we are posted together in Maharlika, I thought.

I had reached the stage where I had shed the awkwardness of being a new didi and had gained more confidence. Having just become an acharya, Didi Asitiima showed eagerness and curiosity about my experiences. I encouraged Didi Asitiima to create a kindergarten in Manila and related some of the history of Ananda Marga's development there. The night before I was to leave on a tour to Digos, where I was to help a new Ananda Marga kindergarten, Didi Asitiima and I sat together on the backdoor steps of the didis' quarters in Mandaluyong, Manila. We enjoyed the warm tropical night and looked at the stars and the moon. After chatting for a while, we sat in silence. Suddenly, she began to cry softly. "What's wrong? Why are your crying?" I asked.

She replied, "Nothing, really. I am feeling sentimental. Can I put my head in your lap?"

"Sure," I answered and moved to let her lean her head down into my lap. I patted her back as she cried.

Afterward, we sat comfortably together and then went inside to sleep. I thought, "When I get back from Digos, I'll try to find out more about why she was crying."

On June 13, 1978, at eight in the evening, while I visited Digos, Didi Asitiima went to the busiest central park in Manila, Rizal Park. She handed out leaflets to many people around her. The leaflets contained a personal message that she had written: "When immorality is dominating all corners of the planet, when righteous human beings become victims of arbitrary misuses, maybe the sacrifice of the innocent human life will burn the seeds and roots of corruption, exploitation, and injustice — the cause of the suffering and degradation of mankind."

When the leaflets were gone, she calmly sat down as if to meditate in that public park, poured gasoline over her body, and self-immolated while reciting a holy mantra. She died quickly and became one of a sacred group of martyrs who sacrificed their lives for Ananda Marga. A local Ananda Marga lay leader, Sister Nandarani, identified her body. She later said, "I couldn't believe it. Her whole body was burned, except her face."

None knew her intention. As soon as I received the phone call telling me of her self-immolation, I believed that her soft crying just a few days earlier arose from the sweet sadness she must have felt knowing she would soon die. Likely, while we looked at the beauty of the stars, the moon, and the night landscape, heard the crickets and other sounds around us, felt the wind, and enjoyed each other's friendship, she thought of how little time she had left. How to treasure your last days knowing soon you won't see, smell, feel, or hear again the world's beauty? How to say goodbye to your colleagues and friends? She wanted, by her sacrifice, to let others know about Baba's persecution in India. The international media had rarely reported about Baba or His years of fasting in jail without bail or a sentence. Baba was held without a conviction because the government knew that he would appeal it to a higher, less locally controlled, court. Didi Asitiima and eight other people self-immolated to force attention to this injustice. Historically, other religious monks and nuns have immolated to bring awareness to others' plight. These people paid the highest price for a great cause and to aid others.

While Didi Asitiima was in Manila preparing herself, I was trying to answer the new kindergarten teacher's question, "What should I teach in the Ananda Marga kindergarten?"

I had an epiphany to use Ananda Marga's evolutionary cycle of creation called "Brahmachakra" as weekly themes to anchor kindergarten learning. I since wondered if there was a connection between Didi Asitiima's end and this educational breakthrough. Is it possible that, like Auntie's elder sister blessing her at her death, did Didi Asitiima had somehow helped me with this epiphany? A little later I talked with my colleague, Didi Ananda Mitra, about tying our curriculum to the evolutionary cycle. Didi liked the idea, and with others she published *Circle of Love*, which became an important reference for Ananda Marga schools. I wrote about it in the published work, *For Universal Minds*.

After Didi Asitiima's death, I stayed in Manila to help calm the local Margiis and to assume some of the work left vacant by her death. During this stay, I helped organize a spiritual program in Rizal Park, at the site where she self-immolated. The program paid her tribute and made the public more aware of Baba's suffering in jail. Every Sunday evening, with a group of Margiis, we chanted and danced kiirtan, followed by meditation, while volunteers handed out leaflets and talked to the public. Our efforts attracted large crowds, between fifty to two hundred people. This program ran regularly for over a year.

One month, my supervisor dada visited Baba in jail and told Him what we were doing. Baba sent back a message to us, "Be bolder and more humane."

I believed Baba was encouraging us to continue raising the public's consciousness through chanting and dancing kiirtan in the park. His words prompted us to be dynamic and moral human beings.

10
First Meeting with the Master

THROUGHOUT BABA'S IMPRISONMENT, He reassured His disciples that dharma (morality) would prevail and He would be released from jail. In 1977, an unprecedented electoral tide swept Indira Gandhi's government out of power. Her ban on Ananda Marga and other organizations was withdrawn by the new government. Consequently, in 1978 the Patna High Court granted Baba a new trial. On July 4, 1978, the court pronounced Him not guilty, and He was acquitted of all charges. In the early morning of August 3, 1978, at long last, they released Baba from jail. Thousands of Margiis filled the streets of Patna to welcome Him home. He broke His historic fast and ate food brought by His elder sister, as He had promised He would. The Indian government's plan to kill Baba and quash Ananda Marga had failed. Before Baba went to jail, Ananda Marga operated in only five countries. By the time He left jail, it had spread to eighty.

As soon as Baba was released, many overseas Margiis and acharyas flew to India to see their guru. I wanted to go but due to my situation in the Philippines I was unable to raise the airfare. Three co-workers, who traveled between different countries and could raise larger amounts of money, conspired together to purchase my airfare. I was deeply moved by their unsolicited generosity and began to work on my legal documents so that I might visit Baba in India.

While I prepared, my supervisors told me that after visiting India I should tour Thailand, Malaysia, and Singapore and should work in these other countries of Southeast Asia. Knowing I would leave the Philippines and work elsewhere, a nostalgic wave struck me. I realized how important the Filipino people had become to me and how much I had learned by living there. Images of the generous families that let me stay with them during my tours flooded my memory. I had become attached to these people and their beautiful country full of green palms and coconut trees swaying in the wind, blue shorelines, and clear tropical skies. I remembered many nights when the young Margiis and I would serenade the stars with devotional songs and Baba Nam Kevalam to guitar accompaniment.

With my papers finally in order, in March 1979 I went to see Baba in Kolkata. My flight arrived in the afternoon and by then Baba had already finished His regular Sunday morning darshan (spiritual meeting) with His disciples. If I had arrived earlier, it would have provided me with an opportunity for my first meeting with Him.

Upon reaching the didis' office and quarters I touched Didi Ananda Bharati's feet and sat on the floor by her bedside telling her of my disappointment that I had missed Baba's darshan and talk. "After waiting so many years, and with Him being so physically near, every hour I wait seems dismally long," I lamented.

She sympathized and told me that her acting office secretary would soon go to Baba's quarters to deliver the didis' daily departmental work report. She gave me permission to accompany that didi and see Baba when He went out of His quarters for His daily field walk.

On this day, after He returned from His morning darshan, Baba kept His quarters free of visitors. Without Didi Ananda Bharati's permission, I would not be able to go there. We reached His Lake Gardens house and found the compound empty except for the individuals that lived there, such as the house guards and His personal assistants. The didis' office secretary turned in the Women's Departmental reports to Baba's assistant. Then she and I stood silently, shoulder to shoulder, on the narrow pathway that led from the side entrance of His house and went to the driveway to where His car was parked. Soon Baba would take this walkway to His car. The car's back seat was specially prepared for Him with a blanket and an Ananda Marga's pratik (symbol) draped along the back cushion. After Baba entered, the driver would then bring Him somewhere quiet for an undisturbed walk.

Right before Baba came out the air became electrically charged. I could feel He would come soon. I became thrilled and kept repeating to myself, "I've waited so long to see you and have worked as your acharya for years, so what will our first meeting be like?"

When Baba came out of the entrance, I saw that He wore all white. He positioned His hands in the Namaskar pose, so I did likewise. I became transported and saw Baba's head and face very clearly. He wore black, slipper-like shoes and His feet looked very distinct. But His torso looked like a swirling mass of radiant light. I thought to myself, you are imagining this. Look closer.

Baba's face and feet were distinctly clear. His body was a flowing cloud of white light. I felt awe as His gleaming body drew near. This is what I might see when I die, I thought.

Baba kept slowly walking forward and stopped directly in front of us. He paused while looking at us and spoke in a commanding voice, "Has the darshan been translated into English? It should be; it must be; it should be!"

While He spoke these words I kept my eyes mostly on His feet, for whenever I looked up I saw the radiant flowing light in place of a torso. Possibly Baba wanted to assure me that this radiant body was real and not a mirage, since He stopped and talked for some moments. Then He walked on and entered the back passenger side of His car. We followed a respectable distance behind Him and watched His assistant close the car door and the car drive out the large, open metal gate.

My mind felt like it was in another world. I went into the main hall of His house and sat for meditation in a large room used as both a meditation and a meeting hall. After about an hour, knowing that Baba would soon return from His walk and I would again have a chance to see Him, I stood along the same path with the other didi, side by side again, waiting for His return. We kept vigil there and did not talk. I did not ask her about her experience of Baba and she did not ask me about mine. We preferred to keep silent, to keep our own inner reflections private. Remembering the stories of other people's encounters with Baba, she may have had the same or a completely different experience than me.

In a little while, the air grew vibrant again and the car pulled in the driveway. Baba got out, put His hands in the Namaskar pose, and walked directly into His house, looking forward and not speaking to us. His demeanor appeared normal, not supernatural, which caused me to relax.

After Baba went inside and upstairs to His room, a volunteer quickly came to us holding a silver metal thermos. The aide said, "Baba is offering you prasad."

Prasad means food or drinks that the guru personally blessed to convey some of His spiritual grace to His disciple. From the metallic thermos into our cupped hands, the assistant poured some young, sweet, coconut water. This extra gesture of acknowledgment from Baba felt like a blessing.

I have reviewed, over and over, what Baba meant by the message He stressed. Darshan means to get glimpses of the Ultimate Truth by observing the spiritual nature of the guru. Most moments with Baba were darshans, moments drenched with an eternal, clear, and divine sense. To be near Baba was to get insight into omniscience, omnipotence, and omnipresence.

What did Baba mean by "translating the darshan into English?" Because I was not a language interpreter I do not think Baba meant it in that way. I believed, initially, that He was encouraging me to write books that translated His high ideals into more easily understandable words for the Western audience. Hence I began writing books on Ananda Marga's education. Luckily, I had encouragement from Dada Vijayananda, who was a principal translator of Baba's talks. In fact, due to his translating work, he earned the nickname "Baba's Pen." Whenever Dada Vijayananda saw me during a visit to India, he would ask if I was writing a book and encourage me to keep at it.

Over many years, after Baba's death, I came to believe that Baba was telling me to describe this darshan and subsequent ones with Him. If I did not interpret His words in this way I would prefer to keep my experiences private, as spiritual experiences are better preserved in secret. Although there existed many persons who knew Baba better and experienced far more than I, likely He wanted His darshans to be described from many perspectives, including those of a Western female disciple. I am thankful that Baba graced me with such wonderful memories.

11
Baba Visits Patna

THE DAY AFTER I finally met Baba in person He was to fly to Patna for a spiritual program. Patna is the Indian capital of the state of Bihar and one of the world's oldest continuously inhabited areas. I planned to join Baba there with a group of didis who would travel with me by overnight train. First, we went to see Him off at Kolkata's Dum Dum Airport. As the airport did not offer any special accommodations, a group of more than twenty Margiis and acharyas gathered in a half circle around Baba who sat in a chair with a blanket draped over it. We looked like a cloud of orange around our guru, who was dressed in white and seated calmly in the main waiting room. He was so charismatic that even bystanders, who were waiting for their flights, stopped to watch Him.

Baba began to say light and humorous things to lift His audience. Then He signaled for Dada Shraddhananda to come closer to Him. Dada Shraddhananda went over and sat on his knees on the floor in front of Baba, keeping his hands in Namaskar pose. I was moved by this touching scene because Dada Shraddhananda was considerably older than Baba and much taller yet he acted as a young boy in front of his beloved father. A person's age, looks, and title does not have any importance between the guru and his disciple.

After Baba's plane departed we prepared for our journey. Before leaving I approached my supervisors to request personal contact (PC) with Baba. They told me that I might be able to have PC in Patna. PC is fully at Baba's discretion. He chooses who will have personal time with Him. Often Baba would inspire and guide during those special meetings. The dadas in the central office would suggest candidates for PC to Baba, but only Baba could choose who He would honor. Acharyas would usually get PC because they were His personal representatives and charged with spreading His teachings.

Each day in Patna my desire for PC grew but it was not granted to me. Instead, I had another interesting experience. At the first Patna darshan, with hundreds of local Margiis in attendance, I began to think that possibly I had not received PC because my heart needed to open more. Up to this point, I was so awed and overwhelmed in front of Baba that these emotions predominated. Instead I wanted to feel love, gratitude, and selfless longing. I wished for tears to roll down my cheeks. Ordinarily, my nature is more stoic and I do not cry easily, especially if anyone else is present. I had often admired the Margii men and women in Maharlika who cried openly with happiness or sadness. I wanted my tears to flow freely like the spring rains nurturing the dry, parched earth.

With these musings in mind, I decided not to make an effort to sit in the front row of the audience where I would be physically nearer to Baba. Usually, I tried to get as close as possible to Him. However, due to my reverie, I felt unworthy and chose to sit at the far back of the crowd. Watching Baba in this mood, suddenly tears came up and flowed down my cheeks. Tears came so heavy I could barely see Him. I felt my heart open and I thought He smiled at me over the crowd as if He knew what I needed and sent loving energy to help.

Baba's mood while we were in Patna was that of a father who returned to His family. The darshan talks He gave there, along with darshans at other places, can still be read in the *Ananda Vacanamrtam* (Blissful Discourses). There are thirty-four volumes of *Ananda Vacanamrtam*.

At the conclusion of the Patna spiritual gathering, I began the journey back to Kolkata. On the return trip, I did not join my colleagues but instead opted to travel alone by a longer train route that would pass by Jamalpur so that I could spend a half day there on my way to Kolkata.

Jamalpur is Baba's childhood home city and the place where Ananda Marga began. It is one of the outstanding places for Margiis to better conjure Baba's youth and the birth of Ananda Marga.

Jamalpur is a small, picturesque city in Bihar State with hills, lakes, and waterfalls. It is best known for hosting India's first and largest railway workshop, which was set up by the British when India was its territory. When my train reached Jamalpur Station I hired a rickshaw driver to take me to the first Ananda Marga primary school ever established, the one Baba had often visited and where Dada Adveshananda had given up his body. There I met a local full-time volunteer who worked in the school. He was unoccupied and offered to be my tour guide and accompany me by rickshaw to various memorable Ananda Marga sites.

Our first stop was at a place referred to as the "tiger's grave." It lay in a vast, parched field that once was a proposed British golf course abandoned before the project reached completion. It lay on the outskirts of Jamalpur. At this location, an Englishman killed a tiger but was killed by the tiger while doing it. Both the tiger and the Englishman were buried near to one another with cemented, rectangular mounds over their graves. Almost every night in those earlier days Baba walked there, usually accompanied by Margiis. Baba would sit on the tiger's grave while the disciples sat in front of Him on the ground. At this spot, He gave meditation lessons and mystical demonstrations. By lantern light, Baba dictated the early foundational Ananda Marga books such as *Ananda Sutram*, *Guide to Human Conduct*, and *Ananda Marga Elementary Philosophy*.

After a while, my tour guide and I continued to the railway quarters where Baba lived with His mother and siblings until, at the request of Ananda Marga in the mid-1960's, He stopped working for the railway department. The Sarkar's home was one of many small, one-story, brick row houses. These quarters were built for the railway employees and their families. In 1944, after the death of His father, Baba left college to support His family and take work, like His father, at the Indian Railways headquarters in the accounting department.

My guide informed me that Baba's younger, unmarried brother, who was not a member of Ananda Marga, still lived at the family house in the railway compound. He knocked on the Sarkars' door and Baba's brother answered. His brother bore a remarkable resemblance to Baba. I said, "Excuse me for disturbing you. I just wanted to see where Baba once lived. I am from the United States where your brother has many disciples. Thank you for your time."

Baba's brother did not speak to me but turned and talked briefly in Bengali to the local full timer. I do not know what was spoken. After that, we went back to the rickshaw. I realized it was time for me to catch my train to Kolkata. We hurried back to the Ananda Marga primary school where I thanked my guide and left. Then I caught the overnight train to Kolkata.

12
Personal Contact with the Master

*B*EFORE I WENT to India, many workers and Margiis who met Baba had shared their personal contacts and experiences with me. Two of these stories stand out, as they were extraordinary and I heard them firsthand. Further, I knew these Margiis well.

The first experience belonged to Brother Ely Latinazo, a local full timer in Maharlika. He kindly helped my transition into the local culture when I first arrived. Brother Ely was middle-aged, mature, and could explain well the Filipino culture. Prior to being a full-time volunteer, Brother Ely was married and worked as an executive in a large company. He became ill, with many chronic ailments, so he sought out Ananda Marga to learn ways to improve his health. Soon, after changing his lifestyle to a yogic one, his condition improved. Brother Ely decided to set aside his marriage and career to devote his life to Ananda Marga as a full-time volunteer.

In 1969 Brother Ely visited India to meet with Baba, who was then living in Ranchi. At this time the Ananda Marga headquarters was located there. This year was very historic for Ananda Marga and is referred to as "The Year of Demonstrations." During Brother Ely's visit, he witnessed Baba perform many miracles. When Baba demonstrated a miracle, He stressed that the occult powers witnessed were not miraculous but were natural. Because they were so rare, people were in awe of them and called them miracles. Baba emphasized that no one should strive to attain occult power as it would cause his or her downfall. Although the occult existed, it was not the goal. In one demonstration Baba boosted a person's clairvoyance, enabling him to see a scene from a past life. Another person, with Baba's aid, entered the mind of an individual living in a country far away. In this state, he described what that person was doing and thinking. To several disciples, Baba gave various states of rapture.

Twice a day, at noon and evening, Baba gave a discourse. Day after day, during the discourses, Baba performed one incredible demonstration after another while describing them like a science professor does to his students. First Baba said to those present, "Sit in a proper posture." Everyone then sat upright in lotus or cross-legged poses. Then Baba selected a disciple to sit in front of Him and told him to do meditation. After a short pause, Baba reached toward the disciple and took hold of him at the back of his neck, at the base of the brain. With Baba's touch, the disciple underwent a dramatic mystical experience. After Baba concluded the demonstration, He stood and fondly spoke to various Margiis while He exited. In His wake, He left an electric charged aura that filled the room.

Each day Brother Ely watched Baba perform these miracles. He hoped that Baba would demonstrate on him. But Baba did not select Brother Ely from the audience to sit in front and be demonstrated on. Each day Brother Ely's desire grew. On the last day before his departure, Baba selected him.

Baba told him to sit in front in lotus posture and begin meditation. Then Baba held the back of his head and ordered the various vital airs of his body to leave, one by one, until Brother Ely's body slumped over lifelessly. Baba called a Margii doctor in the audience to come to the front and check Brother Ely's vital signs. The doctor pronounced that he no longer showed signs of life. Then Baba commanded the vital airs to re-enter Brother Ely's body. Soon he started breathing again and regained consciousness. Baba instructed some acharyas present to massage him and give him warm milk to help strengthen his body after its ordeal. After giving these instructions, Baba rose from the wooden cot He sat on, signaled Namaskar to everyone, and slowly walked out of the room. The spiritual energy in the room was very vibrant and many remained lost in deep meditation.

Brother Ely explained to me, "Dying felt so natural. It felt like I was taking off my clothes and putting them back on. I am no longer afraid of death because of this experience."

He further confided that prior to this demonstration he had personal contact with Baba. While alone with Baba, he received interesting guidance. "Baba told me that I could live to be very old with proper discipline. I could live long enough to witness the beginning of "Sadvipra Samaja," a new moral era on our planet. However, Baba warned me three times to not visit my family, as it would be dangerous for me. What Baba told me has come true. The first time I visited home, I became sick. The second time I went there, I broke my leg. Unfortunately, I have to go again and now I am worried about what Baba has said. But I have to go and solve some family financial matters."

A few days after Brother Ely and I had this conversation, he left to visit his family in Luzon Province and died during that visit from stomach trouble. There were disturbing rumors about the circumstances of his death since his family rushed to bury him before relatives and friends from Manila could arrive. I felt shaken by the loss of this fine spiritual man and I recalled the adage, "A person may or may not do what the guru advises to do. But a person should never do what the guru tells him not to do."

Another Baba experience I heard first hand that impressed me was from a Manila Margii named Brother Ben Cawinian. When Baba visited the Philippines, Ben had personal contact with Baba. While he was alone with Baba he asked, "Please help me have a son so that through my child I can introduce Ananda Marga to others."

Baba told him that his body could not engender a child, which Ben already knew from his local physician. Ben asked for a miracle from Baba as he was newly remarried and they wanted a child. Baba did something during the personal contact that Ben promised

Baba he would not tell anyone. A short time later Ben and his wife, Vina, had a son whom they named Manojit.

I knew this family well. When I returned to Manila after touring the provinces I would visit them. One time I had become very ill with bronchitis while on tour. Brother Ben's family invited me to convalesce for weeks in their home. While I stayed I liked to watch Manojit play. Even though he was three years old, he mostly only said, "Baba. Baba." At four years old he was diagnosed with the rare condition of a tumor next to his pineal gland. Due to its rarity, the doctors treated it for free, as it offered them a chance to study this condition.

Distraught, Ben took Manojit to see many faith healers and physicians for a cure. Ben told everyone he met about Ananda Marga and Manojit's miraculous birth. At five Manojit died. I believe that Manojit was a soul who needed only a short time with us. After Manojit's death, the couple adopted a brother and sister who were around Manojit's age.

When I heard these incredible experiences with Baba, I wondered about my personal contact. Personal contact is not when a guru grants a boon or promises more wealth. Rather the guru knows the disciple's heart and wants to build the character of His disciple and collapse the distance between the disciple and the guru. I did not have to wait much longer for my PC. Upon returning to Kolkata from Jamalpur, I was told that Baba would give it to me the next day.

Usually, men had PC alone with Baba, but Baba did not see women alone due to His impeccable social and moral standards. Instead, Baba saw His female disciples in a small group. I had my PC with a Filipina, Didi Abha, whom I had worked together with in Manila. She had recently finished acharya training after serving some years as a full-time volunteer. We were fortunate to be a group of only two persons.

The morning of our PC, on the way to our central office, I stopped and bought a fragrant white jasmine garland to give to

Baba during PC. One senior acharya named Didi Ananda Giita would accompany us as our guardian. We waited outside His door while Baba's assistants gave us brief instructions. One aide told me, "If Baba is lying down, you should garland His legs. If Baba is sitting, you should garland His neck."

When Baba rang the bell, we entered His room. Baba was in a lying pose, supporting His head with one arm. I gently laid the jasmine garland on His legs. They reminded me of a young child's legs. Then Didi Abha and I went to our knees and bowed. The atmosphere in the room was tender.

Baba rose to sit cross-legged on His couch and we both stood up in front of Him. Baba turned to Didi Abha and asked, "What is your designation and where are you from?"

Didi Abha said, "Hari Pari Mandala Ghosti, Ladies in Cairo Sector."

Baba immediately retorted, "Qahira is the old name of Cairo."

Then He looked at me and said, "What is your designation and where are you from?"

I hoped for some arcane demonstration. I intentionally responded with the word "same" as it sounded mystical to me. I answered Baba, "The same. HPMGL in Manila Sector."

Baba without hesitation responded, "The same because you were born twins in a past life."

When He said this, the aura in the room changed and grew heavy. His comment beckoned the ancient past to enter the room. Then Baba closely looked at us. Our minds were now like a blank slate ready to be filled with His grace. He gestured for us to move closer and we knelt immediately in front of Him. Baba said in a resounding voice, "Glorify your existence through human endeavors. Let this body be properly utilized. This body belongs to the Supreme."

Next, He extended His palms over our heads and said *kalyanamastu*, a blessing that means "you will have spiritual progress."

We bowed again to Baba and my outstretched palms touched His sandals under the couch. Then we stood up, holding our hands in Namaskar pose, and left His room. Didi Abha turned to me and said, "Wasn't Baba smiling beautifully at us throughout our PC."

I turned toward her and said, "Baba wasn't smiling. His face looked quite serious."

We looked at each other. Throughout our personal contact with Baba, we each witnessed a very different expression and mood of Baba. This new wonder made us feel dizzy. He had embodied two different demeanors at once. We walked to the large hall near Baba's room and sat in meditation to internalize and absorb more our intimate time with Baba.

After that, whenever Didi Abha and I met, we did not talk much about our past life as twins. I believed Baba demonstrated to us a chief characteristic of a true guru. A true guru knows the past, present, and future of His disciples. My psychic ability can neither prove nor disapprove whether we were twins in a past life, although it rang true to me. Possible evidence of our past connection may be found in two events that occurred prior to our PC. I once accompanied Didi Abha to spend a day with her family and teach them meditation. She once accompanied my parents when they made a surprise visit to the Philippines to meet me. Dada Adveshananda had instructed her to accompany my parents by bus from Manila to Morong where I was staying. That was a dusty, all-day bus trip due to serious road construction. Therefore, Didi Abha and I met and aided each others' parents. Rarely did an acharya meet another acharya's parents unless they lived in the same country and were active Ananda Marga members. Neither of our parents was involved in Ananda Marga and they lived in different countries.

One last connection we shared was that we both loved working in the field of early childhood education. Like twins, we had similar outlooks.

13
The Master Visits Bangkok

*A*FTER MY PERSONAL contact, I left India and went to help Ananda Marga in Malaysia. My head didi called and told me to fly back to India and represent her at the next RDS (Review Defect Solution) meeting in Kolkata in June 1979. At RDS the departmental heads of each sector met at the central office every other month to discuss their sector's progress. RDS sessions often took place in front of Baba. These sessions allowed Baba to give us targets and monitor our morale, speed, and accomplishments. They were a key strategy to inspire the workers.

I do not remember much about this particular RDS. Primarily, the central office was humming with arrangements related to Baba's tour throughout India and with arrangements for His world tour. It was Baba's first national and international tour since His release from prison.

At the RDS I was told that Baba and an entourage of a dozen senior workers would visit Bangkok and Manila in July or August. I received a list of items that Baba required wherever He visited. Looking at the list, I had new insight into Baba's personal needs. But the length and details of the list left me overwhelmed.

I planned to turn over the list and its responsibility to my female supervisor when I reached Bangkok. However, I learned that she had ceased abruptly being a missionary worker and I had to temporarily assume her duties in Bangkok. Feeling more overwhelmed, I visited the dadas' office to coordinate preparations for Baba's visit. Dada Viirbhadrananda, a very senior worker, immediately assumed leadership. He demonstrated how a seasoned and mature worker took charge of such things. He called various people in Singapore, Malaysia, and Thailand and arranged for them to bring the items, such as new bedding, new dishes, new towels, and others.

On the date of Baba's arrival, in the middle of July, twenty-five members from Singapore, Malaysia, and Thailand traveled to Bangkok to meet Him. Dada Viirbhadrananda suddenly received a call from India with the information that Baba would be delayed three weeks. When Dada Viirbhadrananda told me this I said, "The Margiis traveled from far away. They will be disappointed and frustrated over their expense and effort to reach Bangkok without meeting Baba."

Dada replied, "Don't be dismayed. We will turn their coming into a big retreat and create a vibrant spiritual event."

Under Dada Viirbhadrananda's leadership, we held a three-day meditation retreat. Our retreat's purpose was to send Baba such a strong wave of love that He would hurry to visit us. We hoped that He could not resist our loving efforts. After the retreat, the Margiis returned to their homes rejuvenated and inspired. Three weeks later on August 8, most of them rushed back to meet Baba. For many Margiis, it was their first meeting with their guru.

Unlike the larger gatherings in India, the Margiis' time with Baba would be in small gatherings and intimate. Earlier we had rented a retreat facility for His visit. This second meeting occurred in Shyam Sundar's home. Shyam Sundar was a New Delhi Margii who, with His family, was on a work assignment in Bangkok. They rented a fine, large house there. During Baba's visit, the major events occurred in Shyam Sundar's living room. Baba occupied the master bedroom upstairs and a spare bedroom became the office where Baba met with the workers. Margiis stayed in nearby hotels and workers lived at the dadas' and didis' Bangkok offices.

Before Baba's arrival, we cleaned and prepared the home for His visit. I was in charge of the master bedroom and attached bathroom. While I cleaned His room, I remembered stories of Krishna playing with the gopis, his devotees. They loved to serve and play with Krishna. Preparing His room I felt like a gopi, readying the room for Krishna's arrival. Throughout the cleaning, I cheerfully hummed Baba Nam Kevalam.

During the first night of His visit, Baba met only with the workers in the spare upstairs room. We were around sixteen in number, and we filled up the small room. Baba's mood was light and the atmosphere cozy. He told funny stories that made us laugh and explained about the origins of various English words. One origin I remember Him explaining was, "What is the meaning of 'news'? What is its origin?"

No one gave an acceptable answer so Baba said, "It means information from north, east, west, and south, creating an acronym that became the word 'news.'"

At another point, Baba told us how people were mistakenly using "Baba" e.g. using it in plural form. "This is Baba." "That is Baba." "All is Baba."

He corrected this telling, "Baba is not many. Baba is one."

I felt relief hearing this simple statement, as I had heard quite a few Margiis say, "All is Baba."

The next day Baba gave His darshan talk. There were many duties to prepare for it. Behind the scenes, Didi Ananda Karuna, my direct senior from the central office, supervised the women's activities and Baba's food preparation. His food preparation was an important matter and it was considered a special way to serve the guru. Only very few have had this opportunity. While Didi Ananda Karuna supervised and cooked Baba's meals, I was given the chance to chop His vegetables, wash His dishes, and purchase vegetables for His meals. I remember how Baba enjoyed eating local fruits, fried bitter gourd, fried eggplant, fresh yogurt, and steamed jasmine rice. These duties brought me closer to Baba, like being part of His household. They enabled my mind to be occupied with thoughts of Baba throughout the day, as if life were meant solely to please Him.

Didi Ananda Karuna had assigned me to arrange a group of Margii sisters to dance kaoshiiki and lead it in front of Baba before His talk. A dada was given a similar task of organizing tandava and kaoshiiki to be performed by a group of Margii brothers. These dances were important to Ananda Marga. Tandava was created and first performed by Shiva, the founder of Tantra, but it had stopped being practiced until Baba revived it. Shiva's tandava is a vigorous dance that is the source of the cycle of creation, preservation, and dissolution. The name "tandava" is derived from the Sanskrit word *tandu*, which means "to jump." This dance is performed in a jumping manner by male followers. It has various benefits, such as imbuing the practitioner's mind with courage and determination to fight all types of complexes, even the fear of death itself.

As tandava was a dance for men due to its effect on certain hormones, the Margii women wanted a dance for them. While in jail, Baba had told some female disciples that He would give them such a dance when He was released. Soon after He was released from jail, He created kaoshiiki for the Margii women. Both men and women practice kaoshiiki, but it is particularly beneficial for women.

After Baba created kaoshiiki, He announced that both tandava and kaoshiiki must be performed before any of His public addresses. The Indian government, to harass Ananda Marga, banned the dancing of tandava in public areas because the dancers may use apparatuses like a torch, knife, skull or snake. At Baba's direction, Ananda Marga filed a court petition to gain the right to perform it. It was a lengthy and costly legal battle that went all the way to the Supreme Court of India. There the Supreme Court declared Ananda Marga as a religious denomination per the legal definition, and it had the right to perform tandava in public as part of their practices and rituals. This was a great victory.

During Baba's Bangkok visit, I organized a group of women to dance kaoshiiki in front of Him. To prepare they practiced several times and dressed up in traditional maroon kaoshiiki saris and green blouses. When the time came to dance before Baba, I stood near the dancers and led them by chanting as they danced. Baba watched us intently. Next, a group of men danced tandava and kaoshiiki. After all the dances were performed, Baba said, "very good, very good."

Then He looked carefully over His small audience and began His darshan talk. This talk was the highlight of His Bangkok visit with the Margiis. It was a very special event, as Baba usually gave a darshan talk when many people were present. In Bangkok, we were a small group of Margiis and it was an intimate and homey arrangement.

Baba sat on a chair with the pratik and a blanket decoratively draped over it as we sat on the floor facing Him. He delivered a talk in English on the topic of human logic and sentiment. During the talk, Baba explained that love was essential to human beings, more important than logic. At the completion of His talk, a senior dada asked, "On behalf of the Margiis and workers present will you allow us to perform guru puja?"

Kindly, Baba agreed to this request and we began to sing the ancient chant of devotion where we offer ourselves and our deeds to the guru. At the song's end, we bowed in sweet surrender. Many people started to cry loudly, touched by the tender aura in the room. One Singaporean sister shouted, "Baba!" and leaped into the air to land at Baba's feet. She hugged His legs weeping loudly. We were amazed how far she was able to leap from her kneeling pose. Baba looked at her and gave a big smile. Another didi and I gently pulled her back to a sitting pose. To everyone, Baba said, "As I said, human life is full more of sweet sentiments than logic."

Then Baba stood and bid Namaskar to everyone. We, too, saluted Namaskar to Him and shouted in Sanskrit, *Param Pita Baba Ki*, which means "victory to the Supreme Father," as He left the room.

The next day Didi Ananda Karuna called me and said, "I am busy with the preparation of Baba's food. You will act as the guardian during the sisters' personal contact with Baba."

I was so excited. When the time for their PC came, we entered the room. I bowed and knelt at the back of the room while the sisters rushed to bow and sit in front of Him. Baba wore His customary white kurta shirt and dhoti pants as He sat on a couch in half-lotus posture. Before He began addressing the Margii sisters He looked at me and said, "You are acting as their guardian."

Then He began to inspire and tell each Margii sister to work for the suffering humanity and that they were critical to the uplifting of the downtrodden. Most of the women became teary eyed while He talked to them. When it was over, we bowed and left the room.

At the end of two days in Bangkok, Baba was scheduled for His Manila tour where thousands of members and most of the workers waited to meet Him. We went to Bangkok International Airport to see Baba off. A Thai Margii had reserved a VIP lounge so the Margiis and workers could visit with Baba in private before His departure. In the lounge, Baba sat on a chair with a blanket draped over it. We gathered on the floor in front of Him.

First He talked sweetly to us. He said, "The original name of Thailand was 'Shyam,'" which He said meant "deep green." "Over time it evolved into 'Siam.' Now it is 'Thailand.'"

After Baba talked, the dada requested Baba to allow the Margiis to sing devotional songs to Him. Together we sang, "Baba, please make me a devotee. Baba, this shouldn't seem very much. Just a sprinkle of your divine grace will fill our hearts with hope and the sound of your laughter will give your children bliss. Baba, I offer my whole life to you. Baba, please put me on your divine lap. Baba, please make me a devotee."

After this song was finished, Dada Prashiidananda, who sat directly in front of Baba, led another devotional song. When that song was finished a senior dada called him to the back of the room. His departure created a gap in front of Baba into which I scooted myself. I was now directly sitting at Baba's feet. Another central dada said, "Baba, you are soon leaving. Please allow the Margiis to sing guru puja to you before you leave."

Gracefully Baba agreed and we commenced. Upon reaching the song's last line, *Tava dravyan jagat guru tubhyameva samarpayet*, which means "To you, guru of the universe, I surrender myself," we bowed deeply with outstretched arms. While I bowed, my hands gently touched His feet. Baba responded, "So nice, so sweet."

Then He gave a long Namaskar to everyone in the room. We felt His deep love for us. Then Baba stood up and went with His entourage to the restricted area while we shouted *Param Pita Babaki!* (victory to the Supreme Father) over and over until He disappeared from sight.

After His departure, it was time for the Margiis to go home. A few returned with me to Shyam Sundar's residence to clean up. Dada Viirbhadrananda gave the Margiis permission to take home with them the items they had donated for His visit to keep as a remembrance. For instance, one Margii received the blanket Baba sat on and another kept the towel He had used.

While I was cleaning Baba's room, I saw Baba had left some hairs on the counter. Plus His comb was there. His Personal Assistant had not packed it. I took the hairs and comb to treasure Him and His Bangkok visit. Such items from the guru are dear, as they hold the guru's vibration. Around the world, temples are built to house such relics. I felt very fortunate to have His hair and comb. After finishing my cleaning duty, I left for the didis' office to prepare for my departure to Manila. I was scheduled to join the events there.

At Bangkok International Airport, around 9:00 p.m., I met with a dada who was supposed to be on the same flight as myself. He said, "You need to go quickly and cancel your flight. Baba has been deported from Manila and is presently in the immigration lounge."

Without hesitation, I went to the proper counter and canceled my flight. Then we waited for quite a while for Baba and His entourage to be released from immigration. When they left customs and reached the arrival lounge, Baba immediately returned to Shyam Sundar's home. His entourage went to the dadas' office. One of them recounted their experience at Manila airport: "Even though Baba had previously visited Manila in 1968 and 1969, the Philippine government did not allow Baba to enter. Our sources in the Philippine government told us that Catholic officials and the Indian Consulate both requested the Philippine government not to host Baba again.

The Filipino custom officials did not even let Baba disembark to the waiting room and made Him remain on the plane. When the Filipino Margiis realized the plane carrying Baba would take off with Him on it, they tried to force their way onto the tarmac to stop the plane. Many guards arrived to keep the crowd at bay. Loudly the Filipino Margiis wept when they saw the plane take off. It was a pitiful sight."

The dada continued, "Upon re-entering Bangkok, the Thai immigration official asked for an explanation why the Thai government should re-issue a visa? They were hesitant to reissue a visitor's visa on the same day of departure. A senior Thai immigration official was called over to decide the matter."

Baba told the dada who was acting as His spokesman to tell the officials, "The Philippine government did not understand the proper treatment of monks."

When the senior official heard and saw a dozen orange-robed monks and a nun standing besides Baba, the senior officer granted everyone new visas. The senior official said, "Thailand reveres their monks and knows how to treat them."

As the local organizer of Baba's Bangkok stay, my concern now was the state of Baba's accommodations after many items were brought home by the Margiis as keepsakes. Although Baba surely suffered some discomfort, He did not complain. The only thing his personal assistant said was, "Baba is asking after His comb."

The PA did not know I had it and I kept silent. Earlier I had touched the comb to my head and felt now it was not clean enough for Baba.

That week Baba and His entourage remained in Bangkok and changed their flights to go directly to Taiwan from there. Baba's mood was serious and reclusive. He kept His personal schedule but did not meet with many workers and Margiis during this time. Except for His PA and Didi Ananda Karuna, other workers were told not to visit Shyam Sundar's home. Another didi and I were fortunate to be exempted so that we could assist Didi Ananda Karuna with Baba's care.

These unusual circumstances provided a rare opportunity to serve Baba. While Didi Ananda Karuna and Shyam Sundar's wife prepared His meals, various tasks were assigned to me. At first I tried to iron Baba's clothes but my skills were too poor so instead I ran errands. I brought up and down Baba's meals and washed His dishes. One day Baba left a seed from the chico fruit on His lunch plate which I kept as a remembrance.

My main assignment was to clean Baba's room while He was out for His daily walks. During His absence, I was to tidy His room. When I entered His room, I found its atmosphere holy and calm. Sometimes the room's aura felt light and gentle; at other times it held an atmosphere of purpose and focus. Baba's presence was always tangible.

While dusting the room I did not resist touching His things. One day I took His bathroom slippers and placed them reverently onto the top of my head. Another day I noticed His wooden cane in the corner of the room. Baba's stick is famous in Ananda Marga. By extending His cane to touch a disciple Baba ecstatically transported devotees and did miracles. With the same cane He struck disciples on their palms or calves for wrong doings. I picked up this mysterious cane and rubbed it over my head, back, legs, and arms.

On my last day, while dusting the bedside table, I saw His writing pen and lightly touched it. Maybe it will help me write better, I thought.

My last task every day in Baba's room was to spray it with a fragrant air freshener. Then quickly I would leave His room before He arrived back from field walk. Once I was in the landing in front of His door when He arrived so I quietly stood while He passed by.

The familiarity of being around Baba during His Bangkok stay, combined with keeping Him in my thoughts throughout the day while doing chores for Him, made Him feel like a father. One day when He exited the car and walked toward the house, I reached out without thinking and lightly touched His back. Baba did not say anything and kept walking. I did not know what came over me to do that, as I know it was not proper.

Two days before Baba's departure to Taipei, I flew to Manila to carry messages and reports to our sectorial headquarters. It is difficult to describe how the sweet Bangkok experience contrasted with the bereft Manila situation. The workers and Margiis exuded deep sorrow, anger, disappointment, and frustration. Disappointment and yearning hung in the air. They missed Baba and deeply regretted the loss of the opportunity.

When Baba went to Taiwan, unlike Manila, He was very well received. The Taiwan government offered Baba the same VIP treatment they offered visiting dignitaries. The Taiwan Margiis had a fruitful and exciting visit.

14
The Master Seizes My Acharyaship

*A*FTER REMAINING A few months in Manila, I returned to Bangkok. This was to be my first time to work alone in that field. I struggled to get around on public transport because most of the signage was in Thai script. When I asked for directions only a few people understood English. Each day out meant time spent in traffic congestion, smog, and getting lost. At night the cityscape bustled with night crowds. The new challenges began to overwhelm me and left me homesick for Maharlika.

A few weeks later a group of Taiwan Margii sisters and didis arrived at our Bangkok quarters on their way to India. Bangkok offered cheap fares to India so Margiis from various countries made a layover in Bangkok to take advantage of these fares. The arriving groups were on their way to attend a large spiritual gathering in Patna called DMC (Dharma Maha Chakra). During DMC, Baba would give personal contacts, worker meetings, and darshan.

The visitors were in a jubilant mood. We went together to the dadas' meditation center to enjoy collective meditation. Despite the gay atmosphere, I noticed a creeping trepidation after meditation. It felt like butterflies in my stomach. I shrugged off these jitters and went to sleep.

The next morning upon awakening I noticed that the worrisome butterflies still fluttered. I disregarded them and went about the day, but I felt an unease that lingered in the background. After a couple of days like this, I went with another didi to the local medical clinic.

At the clinic, the Thai doctor diagnosed me as having stress and suggested a sedative. I refused to take any pills and grew more worried. In my youth, my mother had suffered mental illness and I began to doubt myself. Could I follow in her footsteps and have a nervous breakdown? It reminded me of Alice who tumbled down the rabbit hole in the book *Alice in Wonderland*. A small fear was escalating into something bigger. I wondered, How could a meditation teacher have a breakdown? Could I set an example for others like this?

Unfortunately, the visiting didis and Margii sisters left for India, and I was alone with my troubling thoughts. After a few days, I consulted with brother Shyam Sundar, the senior local Margii, who encouraged me to travel to India and talk to my supervisors about it. I thought that maybe they would want to give me a demotion so I arranged for my departure to Kolkata.

When I reached our women's central office, Auntie was the only supervisor in residence. She was too ill to travel with the other didis to be with Baba in Patna. Patiently Auntie listened to my concerns and said, "You must take the train to Patna and attend DMC to let Baba decide what to do."

The overnight train to Patna was very stressful. I was alone with dark thoughts. In my worst hours, I felt claustrophobic in my own skin. Finally, I reached a new level of surrender to Baba. I trust You know what is best for me, I thought, better than anyone else and more than I know myself. I surrender to You.

After I arrived I searched for my Manila Sector supervisors who were surprised to see me. When I told them of my situation and that Auntie had sent me, they advised me to join the DMC until they learned what I should do. There was a large workers reporting meeting with Baba about to start and the didi told me to accompany her.

In a huge tent, hundreds of dadas and didis sat on the ground facing Baba. Our master sat on a beautifully decorated dais, surrounded by a sea of orange-clad workers. I sat next to my head didi, feeling disoriented and in awe. Baba began taking various types of reports from different sectors. Suddenly Baba said, "Manila HPMGL, give your report."

Manila HPMGL was me. No one else. He had singled me out of this large ocean of orange. I whispered to the supervisor next to me, "I'm not here for reporting. What should I do?"

"Stand up," she said, "Baba is asking for you. He knows everything."

I stood up and Baba looked intently at me, while hundreds of dadas and didis stared. Really I did not know what to say. After a couple seconds of silence Baba sternly said, "She is not ready for reporting. Seize her acharyaship," and He made a sweeping gesture with His hand.

Losing one's acaryaship was a grave offense. I was not sure of the full ramifications but it could mean I could not initiate others into meditation lessons on Baba's behalf. Inside I felt stunned. The moment He said, "Seize her acharyaship" something seemed to fly from the top of my head into the air. I understood Baba knew I needed direction like a horse pulling a heavy load. He now had personally taken the reins in His hands.

The next couple of days I walked around like a lost child. People were very kind to me. A Margiis sister from Sydney gave me a massage and prescribed high doses of vitamin B. A senior family acharya, Dada Raghunath Prasad, saw me walking forlornly and invited me into his family tent. He related his remarkable experience during Ananda Marga's conception when Baba told a small group of disciples that He was leaving His body. At this time Baba granted them last wishes. One person pled with Baba to live longer and establish Ananda Marga. I felt grateful to learn from someone who was there on this special occasion.

On the last night of DMC was the major event. After His darshan talk, Baba gave a special blessing and He positioned His hands in *varabhaya* mudra. When Baba gave this mudra the thousands of people there felt an electrical current emanate from Him. The audience became intoxicated. Hundreds wept with joyful tears. Several individuals fell to the ground in trance. Throughout the large tent were loud cries of "Baba! Baba! Baba!" Experiencing the mudra made my spirits lift. I felt fortunate to be there with Baba.

The next night, Baba gave another darshan. After His talk, many people departed to their homes. I felt exhausted and decided to retire. Then around 10:30 a young Indian didi, whom I did not know, aroused me from sleep and said, "We are called to Baba's quarters. We will go in a car that was sent for us because the hour is late."

I was shocked to be riding in a car. Except for an elite few most people walked or traveled by rickshaw to the function. When we reached Baba's quarters it was nearly 11:00 p.m. and Baba was still out on His late field walk.

A handful of workers and a few senior Margiis remained at His quarters. When Baba arrived the senior Margiis greeted Him and together they amiably stood and talked. Then Baba went to His room to eat a late dinner. After forty-five minutes, three Indian dadas, the young Indian didi who came to fetch me, and I went into a small room. We sat on the floor in a horizontal line facing Baba's couch. I was the last one in line. Each of us had lost our acharyaships for various reasons and would receive judgment.

Soon Baba came in and sat down on His couch in the company of the General Secretary (GS). Despite the seriousness of our situation, Baba looked like and acted like a father at home dealing with His recalcitrant children. His attire increased this homey atmosphere. He was not wearing His customary white dhoti. Instead, He now wore a wrapped, green lungi that usually is worn at home after hours. He did not wear His customary kurta shirt. Instead, He wore a white, short-sleeved undershirt. I noticed that his undershirt had a slight moth hole in the front. Seeing Him like this emphasized how much he loved us.

We bowed to Him and then, one by one, starting with the dadas, each of us stood and was evaluated. Baba asked the GS Dada what each had done that caused the loss of his or her acharyaship. Then the GS Dada repeated what Baba had said to the worker. Correspondingly, each worker's answer was repeated by the GS Dada back to Baba. There followed a period where Baba commented on each person's situation and a decision was made. Most of the workers present had lost their acharyaships for arriving late to the function or because they had failed to bring something required. Baba gave some back their acharyaships immediately and others He did not, pending more consideration. I was the last to stand in front of Baba. In my mind, I wondered, "What should I say? Should I tell Him I was not ready or tell Him I was having a nervous breakdown?"

Due to my confusion while I bowed to Baba I thought, Baba, help me know what to say and show me your mercy.

Then I stood up. Baba looked directly at me and spoke first, "This is her first time. Ask her if she will do it again."

GS Dada asked, "Will you henceforward be ready for reporting?"

"Yes," I answered.

Baba said, "As this is her first time, allow her to apply to the Acharya Board for the return of her acharyaship."

Then we all bowed to Him and left the room. Baba had shown me mercy.

The next day I was told to write a letter to the Acharya Board asking to be granted back my acharyaship. A dada supervised this endeavor and dictated what to write. I wrote and rewrote the same request three times over the next two days. I promised that I would not again make the mistake of being unprepared. Each time I submitted a letter to the Acharya Board, the dada would ask me to rewrite it and change a word or a detail. It seemed similar to a child's punishment at school of writing a hundred times the sentence, "I will finish my homework on time." Every letter I wrote made me feel increasingly buoyant. My supervisors told me, "You have your acharyaship back. Baba has confidence in you to go back and continue in your same designation. There will be no demotion or reposting."

After they granted my appeal and I was again an acharya, I flew back to Bangkok. This time I did not stay there but continued to Indonesia via Malaysia. My experience of seeing Baba had not miraculously removed my anxiety but I learned greater lessons. On the train trip to meet with Baba I reached a new level of surrender, and after losing and regaining my acharyaship, I knew Baba believed in me and in my abilities. My situation seemed similar to a soldier on the battlefield. Despite my anxieties, I was expected and needed to continue my duties. The miracle was not the removal of my fears. My miracle was a new strength to endure and face them.

Later more help came from a central newsletter in the form of an article about Baba's recommendations for nervous disorders. The recommendations included the following yoga postures and other helpful practices:

1. yoga mudra
2. diirgha pranama (long greeting)
3. halasana (plow)
4. cakrasana (wheel)
5. extra long shavasana (corpse pose)

The article emphasized that the practitioner should stay in the shavasana pose until he or she became sleepy. This could take as long as twenty minutes. Further, the article advised to have massages and to eat easily digested vegetarian food such as soups and fruits.

I followed all these suggestions, especially the regular practice of long shavasana. Over the course of a year, the butterflies in my stomach lessened and then ceased. Since that experience, whenever I felt significant stress, I performed long relaxation poses. To my relief, the stress would subside before becoming too acute. In this way, Baba cured me of this particular weakness and made me a stronger person.

15
The Master Gives Dharma Samikśa

*A*FTER VISITING BABA I concentrated my field work in Indonesia. Indonesia is an archipelago comprising 17,508 islands, about 6,000 of which are inhabited. The islands lie on the edge of tectonic plates, causing many earthquakes and numerous volcanoes. As it is equatorial, Indonesia has a tropical climate with two distinct seasons, the wet monsoon and dry seasons. Its size, tropical climate, and archipelago geography support the world's second highest level of biodiversity (after Brazil), with a splendid array of Asian and Australasian flora and fauna. It is rich in many natural resources, yet poverty remains widespread.

Even with a republican form of government that has an elected legislature and president, the disparity in Indonesia between the rich and poor is vast. Part of the poverty come from its large population of over 252 million people, making it the world's fourth most populous country. Population alone is not the reason. One cause is the density of population on Java, the politically dominant island. It has an average population density of 940 people per square kilometer (2,435 people per square mile.) Furthermore, the inadequate infrastructure and poor distribution of resources make this density critical. In Java, I made my base and rented a small house. I selected Jakarta, the second largest metropolis in the world, a congested city with vast suburbs.

In Jakarta, I endeavored to meet people interested in learning yoga and meditation and in building an Ananda Marga base. Many Indonesians, particularly the Chinese community, studied yoga at various centers so I contacted these yoga instructors. They permitted me to meet with their yoga students who wanted to know more about meditation.

I also contacted English-speaking organizations like the Rotary Club. These organizations, along with some universities, welcomed lectures on yoga and meditation. To support myself, I taught English as a second language. Often in my English classes, I encountered people interested in learning meditation also.

Besides Jakarta, I regularly toured other cities in Java and Bali to teach meditation and inspire budding Ananda Marga groups. Whenever I traveled to Java and Bali, I stayed in people's homes. By living in their homes I quickly gained familiarity with the Indonesian cultural life.

Since the seventh century, Indonesia had been an important trade region; consequently, it absorbed various cultural, religious, and political models from traders, especially from early Hindu and Buddhist kingdoms. Later, Muslim merchants brought the now-dominant Islam religion there. All these influences were very noticeable. I loved their food rich with fresh spices. Their colorful batik sarongs, gamelan music, and intricate art, often reflecting on themes from the Ramayana and Mahabharata, transported me to a more ancient and classical culture. I noticed an atmosphere of tolerance existed on Java and Bali due to the rich influence of their aesthetic culture.

While working there I began to ponder how to become purer? One day I hoped to become a senior didi, an avadhutika, and dedicate myself more fully. I believed that I still needed to be more dynamic and purer in my thoughts and actions. One day, while I was sitting at home, I listed all the things I regretted doing in my life, from my childhood to the present. I rated the seriousness of each transgression. My plan was to take a self-directed consequence for each wrong action I had committed instead of waiting for nature to arrange a requital.

I decided to do fasting as a form of self-rectification. Generally, my supervisors discouraged workers from undergoing extra fasting.

Workers routinely fasted four times a month as part of their spiritual discipline. Thus additional fasting could weaken the workers' health. Our health was an important asset to the organization. If I was to accomplish extra fasting, it had to be done in secret. My stay in Indonesia provided a good place to undergo additional fasting.

After tallying my indiscretions, I discovered the number of fasting days that I needed to do was thirty-five. Therefore, even if I occasionally did one, this endeavor would take a long time to accomplish. Around this time my Indonesian neighbors started to prepare for their month-long Ramadan fast and they encouraged me to join with them. While deliberating about whether to do fasting, I had a Baba dream that helped decide the course of my action. In my dream, Baba sat on a raised platform in front of many Muslims. The Muslims started their obligatory prayer and prostration to the Almighty Allah. At the back of the room stood Margiis. Baba looked over the heads of the bowing Muslims and emphatically said to the Margiis at the back, "The best of theirs is also Mine."

Awakening to Baba's resounding voice, "The best of theirs is also Mine" felt like a message from Baba to join the Ramadan fast. In this way, I could expediently purify myself.

Ramadan dates varied year to year and are based on a lunar cycle. The exact date was determined when the new moon was sighted. The Indonesian government announced when the fast began and when it ended, twenty-nine or thirty days later. Often it started around the second week of July and lasted until mid-August. The end of Ramadan marked the Muslim New Year, called "Lebaran," and is joyously celebrated like New Year's Eve and New Year's Day. Many Indonesians journeyed great distances to visit their families and to celebrate Lebaran with them.

My month-long fast proved to be more difficult than I had imagined. Unlike my neighbors who were experienced in waking up, cooking, and eating before the 5:00 a. m. sunrise and who were well prepared to eat again at sunset shortly after 6:00 p. m., my schedule made this difficult. I had to do meditation at 5:00 a.m. so I missed the first time to eat. Then I frequently returned late, after sunrise, from tutoring English or attending a yoga class. Therefore I ate only in the evenings and skipped breakfast. Ramadan became arduous, as nighttime provided too little of an opportunity to fully rehydrate and re-nourish.

Indonesian weather during Ramadan was very hot and most places did not have air-conditioning. Public transportation did not have air-conditioning. Fasting was more difficult on the hot bus rides. I noticed other passengers were similarly affected. Usually fellow passengers were gregarious while they rode the bus. During Ramadan, they rarely talked. Rather they went out of their way to be as silent as possible during the daytime hours. They did not want to unintentionally aggravate others or themselves while fasting.

When my regular four times full day and night fasting arrived I underwent these fasts as well. Luckily I was young and in good health. Often I consoled myself that after thirty days of fasting, most of my indiscretions would be cleared from the list. This helped keep my morale up.

For the Lebaran holiday, I decided to visit Bali with a stopover in Surabaya. One of my English students had invited me to overnight in Surabaya at her family's home. I had not previously met her family, but I welcomed the opportunity to meet new people.

On the eve of Lebaran, I began my journey on an overnight bus to Surabaya. The bus departed at 4:00 p.m. and at 6:00 p.m. the passengers broke their last fast on the bus. They began to celebrate the end of Ramadan. I felt light-headed and attributed it to the gaiety of the people celebrating on the bus. Soon though, I grew delirious with fever and fell into a restless sleep throughout the duration of the bus trip.

While in the throngs of fever, I sensed Baba's divine presence and imagined Him saying, "You intended to purify yourself. Now I am gracing you with even more purification."

When the bus reached Surabaya I went to the home of my English student. I had barely finished introducing myself when I fainted from the fever. My fever persisted the next day and at night it worsened. Kindly they took care of me, who was a stranger to them, for a couple of days. Alarmed at my illness's severity they asked, "Do you know anyone who can nurse you, as you need better treatment?"

"Please arrange an overnight train to Cirebon," I replied, "I know a family there who can help me."

That night, despite a high fever, I managed an overnight train ride to Cirebon and arrived very sick on the doorstep of a Margii family that I knew quite well. They immediately sent for a doctor to diagnose my illness. He said, "You have contacted typhoid fever and need specific medicine to get well. I will arrange your medicine for free. This family will take care of you, so just rest and get well."

The Margii family isolated me in their home. They nursed me like they would their own child. When I think of this experience tears of appreciation and gratitude overwhelm me. It took a month to get well. Finally, the doctor pronounced me fit enough to return to Jakarta and do limited work.

Due to my previous month of fasting, along with a month of typhoid fever, I had become very thin and my face had a drawn look. I had earlier informed my higher authorities in Manila about my situation. When they heard I had recovered, they insisted I return to Manila and attend the sectorial retreat and workers' meetings. Over the phone, I tried to get out of going there because I did not feel well enough to work for my fare or to attempt the long journey. My supervisors insisted I could manage and must come. Therefore, with newly improved health, I began to tutor English students and prepare for this trip.

Upon arriving in Manila, when my supervisors saw me, they realized how deteriorated I had become and pitied my condition. They had not fully realized the extent of my weakness. My head didi decided I should not immediately return to Indonesia. Instead,

I should proceed to India and attend Baba's birthday celebration to gain inspiration and grow stronger.

In May 1982, I traveled to India for Baba's Birthday. The celebration took place in a rental hall near Jodhpur Park, Kolkata. The day before and throughout the night, a group of didis, Margii sisters, and I made colorful paper flower decorations. I thought our paper flowers looked humble and very homemade. I thought the decorations should be more elaborate and beautiful. When I told this to an Indian didi who was making flowers with me, she relayed an interesting Baba story:

"One time the Margiis raised money and paid for expensive store-bought decorations for Baba's dais. The event was outdoors and the Margiis wanted the site to look very professional. When Baba arrived and saw the beautifully decorated stage, He made no comment about it. Later that day it rained unexpectedly. The expensive decorations were ruined. Hurriedly the Margiis made new decorations for the stage. These looked simpler and less elegant. When Baba came again to give a talk He lavishly complimented their handmade decorations. The Margiis learned the important lesson that Baba appreciated what they devoutly did with their own hands more than any store bought ones."

In the morning, before the event was to start, a central didi called me over to her. She asked, "Do you have conjunctivitis?"

I answered "No. I had it last week but my conjunctivitis healed. It unfortunately broke a blood vessel in my eye that makes it still look red. But I am no longer contagious."

A week before Baba's birthday an epidemic of conjunctivitis ran through our crowded quarters. Many, myself included, contacted it. If a person was afflicted with conjunctivitis, she could not attend any small meetings with Baba. The central workers wanted to protect Baba from getting sick.

After I reassured the central didi that I was well she said, "Following Baba's birthday celebration, be ready. You might get called by Baba to review your Sixteen Points. This is a new program

Baba has started. During the review, Baba can reveal wrong things you have done in your life. He will give punishment for any wrong actions. This program will lighten and free you of the burden of requital that you owe."

I learned that this new program was called "Sixteen Points Review." Only central dadas and didis thus far had undergone it. There was a strong possibility Baba would extend it on this occasion to overseas dadas and didis. I was informed that during it I would stand alone in front of Baba. He likely would tell various improper actions or thoughts I had committed and give retribution. I thought, It is coincidental I have recently done Ramadan and had typhoid to become purer. Now I will have Sixteen Points Review.

When it was time for Baba's birthday celebration, hundreds of local Margiis arrived. The atmosphere felt spiritually charged. Baba wore a white silk kurta with a white cotton dhoti. His demeanor was generous and loving. He did not give a darshan talk. Instead, He spoke amiably to the Margiis in Bengali.

The personal assistant dada gave Baba a lap tray and tucked a cloth napkin around His neck. Then PA Dada offered Baba some food and drink. Baba took a few sips of the drink and a single bite of food. We watched intently as Baba ate, as we had longed to see Him eat. It had not been long since Baba's years of fasting. He graced His disciples by allowing them to see Him take food.

After the birthday celebration concluded, two overseas didis and I were called into a small room to stand in front of Baba for our Sixteen Points Review. Baba sat on a wooden couch covered with a folded blanket. We bowed to Baba and then sat on the floor in front of Him. Didi Ananda Karuna and general secretary dada were present as our supervisors. Firstly I was called to stand in front of Baba. While I stood I internally prayed to Baba, Do not shame me in front of others.

The thought of any such exposure mortified me even though I could not remember any real grievous action. I knew about my pettiness and some other bad habits. Baba looked intently at me for several seconds. Then He spoke in Bengali to Didi Ananda Karuna. She turned to me and said, "Baba says you are following Sixteen Points so you can sit down."

When I heard what Baba said, I felt relieved. I thought, That was not too difficult. I know my Sixteen Points need improvement. Maybe He is gentler because of my recent fasting and illness. Baba must have heard my plea and so He did not reveal my past actions."

Then Baba called the next didi to the front and He severely scolded her for quite a while. Much of what Baba said was in Bengali, intermingled with a few English phrases such as "unfitting behavior" and "improper habits." At some point, Baba became very angry. He said, "If she wants to remain an acharya, she must grab hold of her central didi's feet. Only if she promises not to do such behaviors again can she remain a didi. Her central didi has to vouch for her as well."

Didi Ananda Karuna vouched for the didi and the didi held her feet repeating, "I will become an ideal daughter of the Cosmic Father and work hard for the suffering humanity."

Now it was the other didi's turn. Again Baba spoke in Bengali. She received a shorter scolding that ended with her promising to improve her behavior. After the last didi had been reviewed, we all bowed and left the room.

Soon after our Sixteen Points Review I returned to field work in Jakarta. Shortly afterward the review program metamorphosed into "Dharma Samikśa." Baba invited all Margiis and acharyas to come to India and receive a similar review from Him. In the historic span of just over three months, Baba used His subtle acuity to grasp the conduct and health of thousands of individual Margiis. Baba had never demonstrated His occult power before to such a large number of people over many continuous days.

On July 25 Baba gave an talk about dharma samikśa saying, "Those who have assembled here are surely good people. Some of you have come all the way from five thousand or ten thousand miles away… In my opinion, Parama Purusa should do something for these good people... So if Parama Purusa should take away some of the sins of the unit beings, they will feel relieved of their heavy load and feel lightened. These people, free from the bondage of 'papa' (vices) and samskaras can do many important works. By dint of their collective efforts, they will bring heaven down onto this terrestrial earth... Hence dharma samikśa is the most epoch-making event of the last fifteen thousand years."

Toward the last days of dharma samikśa, I returned to Kolkata. Primarily I was not sure if the Sixteen Points Review was dharma samikśa. When I arrived, Didi Ananda Karuna told me that I already had it and would not have it again. She explained how tired and sick Baba had become from such a tremendous expenditure of His subtle energies. My visit became preoccupied with concern for Baba's health.

Dharma samikśa, aside from His fast, was the most draining event on Baba's health. Even after dharma samikśa ended, Baba occasionally continued to use His special ability to penetrate a disciple's life and check on his or her character and discipline. His scrutiny could occur during personal contact or any small meeting. Every worker and Margii knew they could not hide a thought or action from Baba. With His all-knowing mind, Baba created and kept external pressure on His disciples to improve.

Many years after this experience I had a chance to meet with the didi that Baba scolded severely at dharma samikśa. It was at Ananda Nagar during a Dharma Maha Samelan program (spiritual gathering). We reminisced about our extraordinary and personal Sixteen Points Review. She said, "During my review, I fell into a trance and felt engulfed by His love. I knew Baba was scolding me, but it felt distant. I had little awareness of what was being said. I do remember my promise at the end to be more ideal."

Then I told her what I remembered of the event. We both had deep appreciation and gratitude for Baba's kindness to us.

16
Field Experience with the Master

AFTER DHARMA SAMIKŚA, I visited India again for senior RDS reporting in my supervisor's stead. Baba's health was still poor on these occasions, as it took Baba months for Him to recover from such extended exertion of His supernatural energy. Despite His weakened health, an interesting event occurred.

At the end of reporting one day, a couple of didis and I waited in Baba's Lake Gardens quarters to see Baba after His routine field walk. As was His habit, Baba would walk alone or with a designated Margii brother or dada. To my knowledge, I had not heard of occasions when a Margii sister or didi attended His field walk. I was therefore surprised when Baba's PA, Dada Ramananda, asked, "Do you want to have field walk with Baba? You should ask Didi Ananda Karuna to arrange it with me."

Later that evening we returned to the didis' quarters and told Didi Ananda Karuna what PA Dada had said. She did not comment or commit to anything after we told her. The next day at Baba's quarters Dada Ramananda again approached and told us to ask Didi Ananda Karuna to talk with him about arranging our field walk. He seemed a little perturbed at our lack of response. We assured him that we were interested, had told Didi Ananda Karuna, and would again talk with her this evening. When we reached home, we told Didi Ananda Karuna what PA Dada said. The next morning she went to Baba's quarters and talked with Dada Ramananda.

On the following, day a small group of us didis drove to Baba's quarters in the Women's Welfare Department car, an old car made before the 1950s, with a large interior. Our car was parked outside of Baba's gate while we went inside and waited. Didi Ananda Karuna warned us to stay close if we hoped to have this opportunity. When Baba got into His car and the gate opened for it, we didis ran and jumped into our car. In our car, there was a driver, five Indian didis, and two overseas didis. Older models of cars could fit more people. In Baba's car, there was the driver and one assistant dada. Our WWD car followed closely Baba's car down the street. One didi told me as we rode, "Baba likes His driver to be smart, quick, and not to stop until He reaches the designated destination."

The opportunity to go on field walk had been a cherished desire of mine. But I never expected it to occur. Now I was following Baba's car to join Him in His outing. Soon the cars reached where Baba wanted to go. The place He chose was alongside a small, man-made lake near the didis' children's home in South End Park. His car had been parked under a row of shade trees and all the doors were open. There were no other people visible in that area of the park, leaving us alone with Baba.

We waited in our car until Baba's assistant signaled us to come out and approach. Baba was not feeling well enough to walk. Instead, He remained seated in the backseat of His car and from there He enjoyed the park's cool, fresh atmosphere.

When Baba's assistant waved us to come nearer, we went and stood by Baba's open door. I noticed His mood was relaxed and He began to talk like a father with His daughters. At first, Baba spoke for awhile in Bengali. Then in English He said, "Do the Margiis in the various sectors enjoy the new *sadavrata* and *paincajanya* programs?"

Didi Ananda Karuna answered, "Yes, Baba, they like it very much and are implementing it regularly."

Baba scanned His daughters and asked, "Is that so?"

In unison, we said, "Yes, Baba. The Margiis like the paincajanya and sadavrata programs."

Then He spoke with His assistant who poured Him a drink from His silver thermos. Baba slowly drank some sips. At this point, the assistant dada gestured us to return to our car. Soon we again followed Baba's car back to His Lake Gardens quarters. Our entire outing was nearly an hour in duration.

The sadavrata and paincajanya programs that Baba inquired about during our field walk were recently instituted by Him. "Sadavrata" meant giving food or other necessary items to needy persons on a regular basis. It was implemented widely. But the more successful program was paincajanya. It was practiced worldwide in our meditation centers and in most Margii homes. *Paincajanya* is a Sanskrit word that means "for five." To Baba, paincajanya meant the Margiis would promptly sing at 5:00 a.m. devotional songs and kiirtan, an uplifting spiritual dance, followed by meditation.

When Lord Krishna lived three thousand years ago He had an occult weapon called Paincajanya. It looked like a conch shell and when Lord Krishna blew it, the sound heartened and lifted the spirits of His soldiers. I believe that Baba had a special weapon like Lord Krishna. His paincajanya weapon was this new program. It generated a strong spiritual wave to fight against the world's crudity. He was particular that paincajanya be done at 5:00 a.m. all around the world, no matter how dark or light that morning hour was.

On December 13, 1981, in Kolkata, Baba spoke about it: "I have introduced paincajanya to help you derive bliss from this state...I want your existence to shine, to be resplendent with the joy of being alive. This is the reason why I introduced paincajanya and sadavrata — to bring supreme fulfillment to your lives." (quoted from from "Ananda Marga Bhagavata Dharma, A Complete Way of Life." http://am-bhagavatadharma.com/about/pa%CC%81in%CC%ADcajanya/)

After this experience, I felt a completeness. Since Didi Ananda Bharati introduced me to Gurukul, I had wanted to connect my life with Baba's life as much as I could. I already felt very fortunate for my opportunity to serve and observe Him in Bangkok. Now after being with Baba on field walk, I felt connected with most of His routine activities; plus I had grown knowledgeable in His ideology. These experiences slowly transformed my fear and awe of Him into sweeter feelings of love and gratitude. I remember once hearing of story where a Margii asked Baba, "Who do you meditate on? In dhyana we meditate on you, so who do you meditate on?"

He answered, "When I meditate I watch my sons and daughters and see how they are doing and if anyone needs some special attention? Can you do this meditation? I do not think so."

The treasured experiences I was having with Baba pushed me to go deeper into my meditative practice and surrender more. I sought communion with Baba in my outer and inner life. But because special events like this field walk were rare, I knew dhyana was my best vehicle to become closer to Baba. So I put more zeal into my meditation effort.

17
Memorable 1980s

*A*FTER BABA WAS released from jail and many followers came to visit Him, the dadas' and didis' quarters quickly became overcrowded. Soon the organization purchased for Baba a larger residence in Lake Gardens, and the didis moved into Baba's old quarters. But these rooms were still too small to accommodate the didis. During reporting sessions and other Ananda Marga events, there was barely walking room at night around the many sleeping forms who lay in rows across the rooms. There were long lines for the bathroom every morning.

The dadas had similar issues. There was a real need for larger living facilities and for larger central office buildings. Thus Baba instructed the organization to locate and buy land for new central office quarters.

Land was found in Tiljala, an outer suburb of Kolkata, on the way to the airport. Two properties were purchased. They were not adjacent but were within close walking distance to each other. The larger land was for the dadas' complex and a future Baba's quarters. The other land was for the didis' complex. Massive fund-raising efforts began globally to raise money for the construction of the buildings.

Building a central office complex was a mammoth undertaking. Especially because Baba insisted on very fast completion of the buildings. To accomplish this, Margiis from around India and from other countries with engineering and large-building-construction experience came to assist. Occasionally Baba ordered the local dadas and didis to physically aid the construction when progress was not going fast enough. The old saying, "It happens with blood, sweat, and tears," was true when creating the dadas' and didis' central office complexes.

The size of the multistory buildings was impressive. Each compound had a large meditation hall built next to each complex that could sit hundreds of people. These buildings were well-constructed, well-designed spaces. As soon as they were livable, even though they were not nearly complete, the local central workers moved in and construction continued around them.

My sector did many fund-raising activities for the new central office and encouraged Margiis to donate to India for the construction costs. It was an important task for us.

When I went to India while construction was going on I was amazed at how quickly and efficiently the central offices were built. It was pleasant to live in them. Each sector had their own rooms to use while they stayed at the central office. Central office workers had their own offices and quarters. These rooms had adjoining bathrooms and a little veranda to be used as a cooking area. The buildings now reflected our mission's needs by the grandeur of these dwellings. We had high-rise buildings.

In the joy and excitement of adjusting to our new living compounds, tragedy struck the workers. Sixteen monks and one nun of Ananda Marga were brutally killed on the morning of April 30, 1982, after many workers had traveled to Tiljala for an education conference. In three different locations at Bijon Setu, near Ballygunge, hoodlums waited and struck at any orange-robed Ananda Marga worker that passed. Seventeen workers were dragged out of taxis that they were taking to our Tiljala headquarters, beaten to death, and then set on fire. It was witnessed by hundreds of people, but despite the attacks being carried out in broad daylight, no arrests were ever made.

The police suggested it was a mob reaction due to rumors of Ananda Marga engaging in child kidnapping. These were false accusations that occasionally were spread by corrupt persons to counter Ananda Marga's influence in the local area. The didis had established a children's home on one floor of their headquarters. All the children were orphans or had been turned over to Ananda Marga by parents who were financially incapable of raising them. The real reason for the massacre was that corrupt persons alarmed at Ananda Marga's amazing growth organized and paid the killers. The new buildings threatened local leaders. They especially hated us due to our pro-PROUT and anti-communist stance. Our new offices in Tiljala were situated in a communist-ruled area. So they often spread vicious rumors.

After repeated calls for a formal judicial investigation, a single-member judicial commission was set up to investigate the killings in 2012. Until the present, there has been no justice attained for the victims.

I arrived in Kolkata a couple of weeks after the massacre. Their grief and shock were palatable. I met with one of the didis who was clubbed by the hoodlums but survived. It filled me with horror to see such a fine young woman suffer like this. For the first time during this great endeavor, the joy and strength I felt at our successful building were mixed with the bitter loss of fellow workers. We developed new vigilance whenever we went out and we changed our travel route to Baba's quarters. However, Ananda Marga was resilient and Baba inspired us to move forward.

For the most part, visiting Baba and living in the Tiljala central office in the early 1980s was very pleasant. One event I remember happened during a visit in January 1982 when I was in India for reporting and for the DMC function at Ananda Nagar. After the events were finished, Baba and many of us returned to Kolkata. We stayed in Tiljala but Baba stayed in His MG quarters at Lake Gardens, as his quarters in Tiljala had not been finished. He had instructed to complete the central offices first. It was on this occasion I saw Baba without eyeglasses.

Previously, whenever I saw Baba, He always wore thick eyeglasses. Due to His poisoning in jail, His eyesight had been severely compromised and He wore very thick lenses. To see Him without His glasses intrigued me because I had heard various stories about Margiis who had looked directly into Baba's eyes. One Margii sister said, "I saw the universe with its myriad stars and planets swirling inside the depths of Baba's eyes." Devotees loved to share such stories and there were many of them.

One early evening when Baba returned from field walk, He exited the car without wearing His eyeglasses. I could not see directly into His eyes but felt thrilled to see Him without eyeglasses. After Baba walked into His house, His assistant ran back to the car and retrieved the eyeglasses for Baba. Apparently, He had left them behind. I chuckled inwardly at how this action had fulfilled another secret desire. It felt like there was a sweet flow between Baba and myself.

Another personal milestone occurred around this time when I initiated a conversation with Baba. Up to this moment I had only responded to His questions during personal contact and in reporting sessions. I had not questioned Him on anything. In His presence, I usually felt too awed and too overwhelmed. But during this visit, prompted by frequently hearing how Baba was not in good health, when He returned from His field walk I asked, "How are you today, Baba?"

He answered, "A little bit better."

Then, together with others standing next to me, we sighed, "Aah."

In regards to Baba's health, besides what I was told, I had developed my own system of categorizing the stages of Baba's health. During my first visits, after His long fast in jail, Baba did not wear socks. He sat barefoot or walked in shoes without socks. Later, sometime after His world tour, I noticed that Baba regularly wore socks. When I saw this I missed His bare feet. It signaled to me that His health was weaker. Lastly, sometime after dharma samikśa, I saw that He used His cane to help Him walk. Although I noticed these changes, overall, I believed that Baba was quite hardy. I did not fully absorb the seriousness of His escalating heart ailments.

Near the end of my visit this time I had to buy a train ticket for my journey home. I left early in the morning and hurried on my errand so that I might return to Baba's quarters before He left for field walk. While waiting for my last bus transfer, the bus took very long to arrive. I knew I would not reach Baba's quarters in time to see Him leave or return from field walk. Standing on a busy Kolkata street corner, I felt sad and dejected. Suddenly I spied Baba's car. He was on His way to field walk. The car turned the corner where I stood at the bus stand. I saw Baba sitting alone in the backseat through the lowered window. The sight of my guru made me ecstatic. I believed Baba timed His route so I would not be disappointed.

Another special experience occurred the day I was leaving. I bought a fragrant white jasmine garland in the market to offer Baba when He returned from His field walk. My supervisory didi said He might accept it as I was leaving to return to my post. Otherwise, if Baba did not receive it directly, His assistant would take the garland and put it in Baba's room to make it fragrant.

I waited on the side of the driveway, near His entrance, for Baba's return from field walk. When the car pulled in the driveway and Baba left the car, I held out my garland toward Him. Baba put out His hands and took the garland. While reaching for the garland, He touched both my hands with His and looked at me while asking, "And who has betokened this?"

I replied, "Didi Nandita, Baba."

Then He handed the white flowers to His assistant to carry inside.

At that moment I flashed back to an earlier discussion with a Margii sister in Kuala Lumpur named Pranadevii. She had told me of an experience in which she had offered a garland to Baba and He had touched her hands. Pranadevii insisted that her heart had become kinder toward others since His touch. As she related her experiences I remember making an inner wish that day. My wish was that Baba might touch my hands. Therefore, when Baba touched both of my hands, I felt grateful that He had fulfilled another desire.

Being in the presence of a charismatic person like Baba, metaphoric thinking bubbled up. As Baba was so sacrificing and concerned for others, bowing to Him was bowing to every man and woman. His hands, indeed, were symbolic of extending a hand to those in need. The touch of these generous hands helped me to become kinder.

Outside Baba's quarters at Ananda Nagar in the 1980s

Baba at DMC in Ananda Nagar

18
Neo-Humanism and Songs of the New Dawn

*I*N 1982, WHILE I was in Manila Sector engaged in field work, I learned from those who had visited Baba recently of two new major developments. Baba had introduced the philosophy of Neo-humanism and had created Prabhat Samgiita (songs of the new dawn).

Neo-humanism is a philosophy that encourages people to love and care for all beings, both animate and inanimate. Baba believed in an all-encompassing kindness. He encouraged us to seek universal love because such expression enables us to touch the wellspring of perennial inspiration. To aid humanity's quest for universal love, Baba devised a technique for better discernment called "proto-psychic-spiritual structure." This technique connects rationality with compassion. One simply asks the question, "Does this idea or act employ universal welfare or not?" Rationality yoked with the concern for universal well-being creates a measuring stick to influence important decisions.

Baba stated how neo-humanism should be implemented. The speed, He said, must be revolutionary and not reformist or reactionary. A revolutionary zeal for change applied to every arena of life — politics, economics, education, art, and science. Good changes needed to be done as quickly as possible.

When traveling in my field, I began teaching neo-humanism to the local Margiis. I thought often about it. I was especially excited to utilize neo-humanism in our schools. We could choose words, behaviors, curriculum, and resources that were more neo-humanistic. In just a brief time, neo-humanism was broadening my outlook and increasing my compassion.

The other great development Baba gave at this time started September 14, 1982. Baba introduced Prabhat Samgiita (Songs of the New Dawn). Until His death, He composed both melodies and lyrics for 5,018 songs. Baba created a new school of music and dance. The number of songs He composed surpassed those of Nobel Prize winner, Rabindranath Tagore, who had previously written the most songs. Every one of Baba's Prabhat Samgiita is poetic, full of beautiful imagery, and positive. Often the tunes incorporated ancient melodies from various countries, reviving forgotten airs.

Most Prabhat Samgiita lyrics are in Bengali, with a few in Sanskrit, Hindi, and English. Around the world, Ananda Marga members began to learn and sing His new songs. We were drawn to the songs' optimism and devotion. Because Bengali is very similar to Sanskrit, singing Prabhat Samgiita vibrated us like Sanskrit did.

At each RDS meetings in our sector, a time would be designated for classes on the new Prabhat Samgiita songs. The first song we learned that Baba composed was "Jyotirgiita." Its translation is:

> O Lord, lead me on. Lead me unto the fountain of effulgence. O Lord, lead me on. I can no longer bear the pain of darkness in my heart. With Your songs, break my deep slumber. O Lord, lead me on.

When I next visited India, I discovered that Prabhat Samgiita had changed our routines with Baba. During my visit, I frequently heard Baba ring His bell. Ringing it once called His personal assistant and ringing it twice brought His second PA. Ringing it thrice meant Baba would dictate a new Prabhat Samgiita. A group of workers, chosen for their literacy in music and notation, were given the duty to help Baba with Prabhat Samgiita. When Baba rang three times they would enter His room. Baba would sing first the new tune, followed by its lyrics. After they wrote and annotated the new song, they would sing the new song back to Baba and He would correct any errors. Then they would leave His room, record it, and teach others. In this manner, Baba often composed up to five songs a day.

Usually when Baba left His house to go on field walk or returned from it, those in attendance would sing Prabhat Samgiita to Him. Often the beauty of the moment propelled Baba to pause, listen, and ask, "Do you like this new song?"

"Yes, Baba," we would answer.

"Should this song be kept or should it be torn up?" He would ask while pantomiming tearing it up to induce our mirth.

"Keep it, Baba," we would vigorously tell.

"Acha," He would reply while moving His head side to side affirmatively.

Then He walked on with His hands held in Namaskar pose while we serenaded Him with Prabhat Samgiita until He was out of hearing distance. His aura, the music, the gardens and the comradeship transported us to sweeter and deeper heights.

After Baba introduced Prabhat Samgiita, they became part of most reporting sessions. Before Baba started taking our reports we would sing Prabhat Samgiita to Him. Then after reporting finished, we frequently sang another song to Him. During weekly darshan talks with the Margiis, Prabhat Samgiita was led by a good singer accompanied by a harmonium. Prabhat Samgiita often was sung whenever a small group of Margiis or workers gathered. In this way our hearts grew sweeter and more blissful.

During one RDS in Kolkata, after Baba's evening field walk, the car would not pull into the driveway but remained on the street. Someone placed a chair in the driveway for Baba to sit upon while we plumped ourselves down on the pavement at His feet. Surrounded by His gardens, under the moonlight, we serenaded Him with Prabhat Samgiita. These are my favorite memories of singing Prabhat Samgiita to Baba. I entered a deep and sonorous mood while sitting and serenading Baba at His feet in the shadows of His lush garden lit by moonlight.

One night when Baba returned from a field walk, we began to sing for Him Prabhat Samgiita. But Baba did not sit. Instead, He stood and began to speak to us in an ancient language which had many deep and unusual sounds. Then He said, "This language has not been heard for over ten thousand years."

Continuing in a deep voice, Baba said, "The moment you first came in contact with Parama Purusa (Supreme Being) is so hoary that it CANNOT BE REMEMBERED." (He elongated the pronunciation of these last words.)

Then Baba went inside His house, leaving us dizzy from the antiquity and intuition vibrating in the night air.

19
His New Garden Program

*I*N ADDITION TO neo-humanism and Prabhat Samgiita, Baba implemented a new garden program. He wanted to accelerate our neo-humanistic appreciation for all kinds of life and to broaden and accelerate our care of plants. Anyone visiting Him was ordered to bring with them five plants for His garden. If they did not bring the plants, they could not meet with Baba.

Devotees all over India and from other countries arrived with plants. Often central office would send lists of specific varieties that Baba requested we bring Him from various regions of the world. I, like others, had to search and get certain plants from Malaysia and Indonesia. This forced me to learn more about the flora and their care in my field.

On one occasion I heard Baba wanted a rafflesia flower from our sector. This flower grows exclusively in Indonesia, Malaysia, Thailand, and the Philippines. It first was discovered in the Indonesian rain forest. The plant is parasitic and has no stems, leaves, or roots. The only part of the plant seen outside the host vine is a five-petaled flower that may be over one hundred centimeters in diameter and weigh up to ten kilograms. Most unusual is its smell, which is like rotting meat when it is in bloom. A blooming rafflesia is rare to see.

On hearing about Baba's request, we who were working in Indonesia made inquiries about bringing a rafflesia to India. We learned quickly how rare it was and that we could not do it. However, the effort awoke in us new knowledge and we brought many other plants from there.

When Baba received the plants, He gave each plant its own Sanskrit name, instructed where it should be planted, and what was needed for its care. The plants were then tagged with their popular names Latin names and Sanskrit names. Many stories circulated about how Baba frequently doted on His garden. He would know while sitting in His room if a specific plant had not received water. The attention and care Baba lavished on His plants set an example to everyone. Sometimes I wondered, Is He choosing a new cadre of disciples for a future lifetime? Will these plants one day evolve to the human level and serve Baba?

During this period, when Baba would not see us without bringing Him at least five plants, we had to sometimes go through extreme circumstances to get them there. Through all our efforts, thousands of plants arrived from every corner of the world. Soon His gardens had more varieties of certain species than any other garden in the world.

Baba began to invite Margiis for a garden tour program. In small groups, Baba would show Margiis His garden and explain to them various historical and botanical data. This gave the Margiis an opportunity to be close to Baba. I did not get this opportunity but Didi Ananda Karuna, who was busy organizing the hundreds of plants that arrived daily, allowed me to work in the back rooms of the greenhouse. I prepared the plant tags and removed dying leaves. This provided me with some insight as to Baba's meticulous care of His garden.

Neo-humanism propounds that plants and animals are equally as important and precious as human beings. Existentially our value is the same, but utilitarian-wise we differ. To Baba, every plant deserved proper care and love just as human beings did. Humans were not, as in other philosophies, loftily standing apart from creation. Flora and fauna were not treated merely as commodities. To be a neo-humanist meant to exhibit pervasive love and, like the sun, shine equally on all. Baba repeatedly demonstrated universal love. In fact, He stressed that human beings have the duty to be caretakers and to protect other species. Through Baba's plant program, His disciples rapidly expanded their love and awareness of plants, animals, and the environment.

20
Discipline Experiences While Reporting

With Baba giving us so many new philosophies and programs while He demanded increased and varied types of service, we often failed to please Him. Thus workers frequently met with reprimands from Baba. I, too, received various rebukes from Him.

Throughout India's history, gurus used various methods to pressure and accelerate their disciples' progress. According to Tantra, there are three types of gurus. The inferior guru gives inspiration and speeches but does not scold or follow up the disciples' progress. Mediocre gurus impart wisdom and encourage discipline, but they are not too demanding about whether the disciples follow that discipline or not. Superior gurus provided meticulous instruction and inspiration and make sure their disciples improve through various circumstantial pressures. Often these gurus mete out difficult tasks, corporal punishment, and keep a sharp watch on their disciples.

Like gurus, there are three types of disciples. The worst disciples visit their guru for inspiration, but away from their guru they quickly forget the practice. Middling disciples retain much of what the guru gives, but when left on their own they slowly lose everything. The best disciples follow the guru and his teachings throughout their lives, regardless if the guru is present or not.

Baba was a superior guru who demanded a high level of discipline from His disciples. Because He had so many disciples, Baba created systematic practices for them to do. Along with this, He organized a global mission with hundreds of teachers to represent

Him and provide circumstantial pressure in His stead. I believe it was paramount for Baba to create a fierce disciplinarian environment while He was alive. After His death, His disciples would be clear about what He required of them.

Many followers who met with Baba found that He acted like a tiger when it came to their discipline. If they had done wrong deeds, He sometimes exposed them. If they did not follow their discipline, He corrected them. If they did not serve enough, He showed His disappointment. To be groomed in this way directly by Baba was considered a blessing, no matter the reprehension.

Tantra gurus like Baba lessened their disciples' burdens through these punishments. It is said that each strike of a guru's cane can lighten a disciple's load and hasten their liberation. Most of Baba's workers felt blessed to receive His scolding, although at the time of receiving the scoldings, Baba's fierceness could overwhelm them.

Baba invented so many ingenious ways to rebuke us that history will not be able to record them all. Many individuals who experienced them, primarily during reporting times and during the dharma samikśa program, have shared some of their experiences.

Throughout my time as a sectorial representative, I experienced various reporting sessions with Baba. Part of the reporting sessions usually contained scoldings for either my individual organizational output or my sector's Woman's Department unaccomplished work. My first punishment from Baba in 1979 was "tic-tics." I crossed my arms over my chest, held my ears with my opposite hands, and repeatedly squatted up and down. While doing tic-tics, I felt childish and regretful for disappointing Baba.

At the September 1983 RDS I experienced heavier corporal punishment. This may have been due to my attending a senior RDS, which were usually aimed at the chief sectorial representatives. My supervisory Indian didi was designated to attend but due to circumstances she asked me to go in her stead. The RDS was focused on each sector's output. Only two of us didis were not an Indian head didi.

Baba was in a severe mood. The didis went together as a group to Lake Gardens to give their report in front of Him. Each didi, one by one, stood alone in front of Baba and answered questions about her sector's progress. If the sector had not shown significant progress, Baba would command the GS to moderately strike the back of our calves with Baba's cane. Every time GS struck He asked questions like, "When will you establish a new school." "When and where will a new children's home be created?"

After a few questions like these, Baba indicated for GS Dada to stop and do the same process on the next worker. Every day we endured this, again and again. The first couple of days it did not hurt. After a few days of being struck, even moderately, in the same spot on the calves, it began to smart. Even worse, we saw how unhappy Baba appeared. It made us didis very sad. Our group became sensitive to His scolding and His disappointed mood. At this point, a mild reprimand from Baba and one tap of the cane brought us to tears. As soon as we showed tears Baba immediately softened and stopped scolding us. Every reporting session ended with a bow. When we left His room we talked among ourselves about Baba, the work, and how to accomplish the targets.

In the 1980s Baba gave many new psychological reprimands to the women's department. I recall Baba telling the dadas in the room, "They act like "living luggage."

He continued with His scolding by saying, "They are busy gossiping instead of doing service work. Gossip for the didis is like eating rasagullas (a well-known Indian sweet)."

While He made these comments, Baba pantomimed eating sweets.

Next, Baba asked us to stand and walk across the reporting room. We enacted being village women carrying large pots called *matka* on our heads. While we did this, Baba said, "They behave like women who go to the marketplace to gossip instead of doing their missionary work."

Although most of Baba's scoldings were in Bengali, I could understand some of it as He often included a few English phrases and used hand gestures. Usually, one Indian didi would whisper brief translations to the overseas didis as well.

At the end of the 1980s, Baba gave the worst punishment to our department. He refused to take any reporting session with us. During one year, He would often grow so angry in the middle of our reporting session that He would end our reporting immediately and dismiss us. We thought this type of retribution was by far the worst. To be deprived of His presence and attention was extremely painful to us.

Baba created many pleasant and funny discipline moments as well. One lighter reporting session I remember went like this:

We waited in the large meditation hall while Baba was upstairs in His room taking various meetings. A rumor spread how angry Baba was at our lack of progress. We were warned that Baba would be very serious when He took our report. Suddenly, we heard Baba ring His bell. PA Dada called, "All workers report upstairs."

Dadas and didis rushed up to the small meeting hall outside Baba's bedroom. We bowed to His closed door and stood to wait for Him. Soon Baba exited His room. He wore on His feet very thick, fuzzy, pastel slippers that a devotee had gifted Him. The ridiculous looking fuzzy slippers were incongruous with a serious reporting session. We laughed inwardly and knew that Baba was playing with us. We could not believe Him to be serious while He wore such funny slippers.

That reporting session stayed lighthearted and we said to ourselves, Baba missed us and used the excuse of reporting today to spend time together.

During another RDS Meeting, the reporting dadas and didis began to arrive at Baba's quarters later and later each day. We were officially told to arrive at a specific time but we observed that RDS was not actually starting then. Our presumption was that we could arrive later.

One day when we reached Baba's quarters the gate was closed and locked. No one could enter the compound. Standing outside on the street we asked Baba's volunteer guards, "Why can't we enter?"

They replied, "Baba ordered the gate locked because you were late."

Soon a sizable group of workers stood outside His gate. The small door in the middle of the big metal gate finally opened to let the workers enter. But, due to the small size of the door, it allowed only one worker at a time. I was very near to the gate's door when it opened so I was the third person to enter. I took off my shoes and went inside the front door of the big darshan hall.

Upon entering I saw Baba was seated on a chair at the front of the hall awaiting us. I went to my knees and bowed to Him. Then I sat down to wait for the other workers. What I noticed was Baba had created a circumstance where He could watch each worker bow to Him, one by one. What seemed a rebuke turned into a devotional gift of individual attention. After everyone had entered the hall, we sang Prabhat Samgiita to Him. There was a brief bit of reporting, and then it ended for the day.

Another funny event occurred during DMC at Ananda Nagar. It was a large DMC with over twenty thousand disciples. The workers had come from throughout India and other countries to attend reporting and the spiritual functions. Baba led the worker's reporting sessions after His darshan talks. A medium-sized tent had been erected near His quarters to keep this reporting private and separate from the main events.

Baba gave instructions that workers should reach the reporting tent before He did. If they failed to arrive on time they risked losing their acharyaship. This caused us to rush as quickly as possible after each darshan talk from the main tent to the smaller tent near His quarters. We found clever ways to speed this up. Instead of leaving our sandals outside the darshan tent, as was customary, we hid them in our shoulder bags. It saved us precious minutes of searching for our slippers.

As soon as Baba left the dais, we jumped up and ran toward the workers' reporting tent. Meanwhile, Baba took a circuitous route there in His car. Senior and junior, young and old, male and female workers ran. While running in a long line of workers along the dusty paths, under the moonlight and under the hot son, I felt that we were His children and equal in His care.

Each day when Baba arrived there would be a few workers entering at the back of the tent. Some squeezed under the sides of the tent. Baba graciously pretended He did not see them. So no one lost their acharyaship.

21
Flooded Quarters

*I*N TILJALA, AFTER the dadas' and didis' compounds were mostly completed, a new Marga Guru (MG) quarters was built there. Once it was ready, Baba took up residence there instead of at His Lake Gardens quarters. I liked His previous residence but quickly adjusted to seeing Him in His new quarters. The workers enjoyed that He now lived in the same compound. We felt relief that He would be safer there. His previous home was a large, pre-owned house in the middle of a residential area. This one was built for Him and had a design that looked like an "M" for Marga Guru.

But in May 1984, after DMC in Ranchi when Baba returned to Kolkata, there were torrential rains and subsequent floods. The dadas', didis', and Baba's quarters became flooded. Our compounds sat next to large ponds that overflowed with the heavy rains. The nearby village also flooded and its inhabitants were evacuated to higher grounds. In our offices the first-floor residents moved upstairs. However, it was thought that for Baba's safety He should temporarily stay at His Lake Gardens quarters. To transfer, Baba had to leave by boat.

Evacuating Baba was a touching scene. He sat in a rowboat while several dadas waded into chest-high water and pulled it for blocks until they reached higher ground. There Baba was driven to His Lake Gardens house. From our quarters I could see Baba get out of the boat and drive away.

Because the didis' quarters was so flooded it was difficult for the inhabitants to leave. Most waited out the flood on the second and third floors. A few of us overseas didis did not want to miss visits with Baba during the floods. We waded in chest-high water out to the main road. While wading, we joked with each other not to look closely at what might be in that dirty water. At the main road we hailed a taxi to bring us to the smaller former didis' quarters, which was now used as a children's home. I was surprised at how small it looked after growing accustomed to living at our Tiljala quarters.

After we didis transferred to the old quarters, we visited Baba every day. He took regular reports from the central workers about their relief work for the victims of the flood. Daily Indian dadas and didis distributed hot food to the people. Ananda Marga assisted the evacuated villagers who lived in our area and had been stricken by the floods. This helped to improve our standing in the local area.

22
I Become an Avadhutika

NINETEEN EIGHTY FIVE was a spectacular year. Over time I had considerably improved myself and curbed my worst character traits. I particularly lessened displaying anger, which Asians considered in poor taste. My confidence and social skills had grown.

More importantly, meditation had become increasingly introspective and deeper. Devotion was the key that unlocked special meditation. Meditation became more important than anything else as my way to connect with Baba wherever I was.

During the past three years I had centralized my missionary work in Jakarta and was maintaining a kindergarten there. Another didi had started the kindergarten and when she was transferred, I moved there to keep it going. The kindergarten was in a rented house located in an overcrowded suburb in the heart of Jakarta. Oddly, this suburb was adjacent to a wealthy area with many consular offices. The school's suburb was a series of alleys with too many small houses on it, huddled closely together and with only pathways around them. The large maze of rows and rows of houses reminded me of a giant ant farm that I once saw in a science class. Thousands of people living in a small space.

My rented house was fairly good sized. It had two bedrooms, a living room, and a large attached room that was used for the kindergarten. To expand the kindergarten's space, I allocated the living room for the kindergarten as well. Twenty-five children could be comfortably accommodated. The children paid a small fee that went toward the teacher's salary, which was also supplemented from my earnings tutoring English. Tutoring was my main source of income in Jakarta and was a good way to raise funds. It also provided a means to meet more Indonesians.

One day, in the early morning hours, I had a Baba dream. In my dream, Baba said, "Your landlord will be helpful to you."

I awoke surprised to have Baba mention in a dream my landlord, but the aftermath of seeing Him filled me with a sense of well-being. I lingered in my bed wondering at it. Suddenly I heard a loud bang and thought, the house across from mine must have had an explosion.

I dressed quickly and went outside to see what happened. The neighbors were standing outside their house looking at mine. "Your schoolroom's ceiling has collapsed," said my neighbor. "Is your electricity off?"

Together we went inside and carefully removed the fuse from the circuit box to prevent a fire. Then, accompanied by a local friend, I went to meet the landlord and inform him of the situation. Inside I felt quite shaken by the experience but I hoped that the recent dream indicated the landlord would help.

The landlord was a local Hadj who enjoyed considerable respect. I explained to him via the interpreter that the ceiling had collapsed. He said that the previous didi had asked his permission to remove a post in the classroom, as she wanted more space for the children's desks. Now he realized he was wrong to have given her permission, for undoubtedly the post had supported the roof. Its removal had caused the roof's collapse. He assured me he would assume the cost of the repair and do it quickly so as to not disrupt the school's operation for too long. True to his word, within three weeks the school smoothly resumed after the needed support beam was restored.

In April, after this incident, I received a phone call from my head didi. She told me that if I wanted to become an avadhutika I must reach Kolkata in two weeks' time. Baba had given a list of names and my name was on this list. I had hoped for many years to become an avadhutika. These advanced monks and nuns practiced a special meditation that aided their efforts to go beyond worldly concerns like family, clothes, and wealth, in order to focus more on God and the upliftment of others.

I arranged my flight from Jakarta to Singapore, rode a train to Bangkok, and flew to Dhaka in Bangladesh. My decision to fly into Dhaka instead of directly into Kolkata was due to a fear that the immigration officials might ask why I was returning so soon to India? What was the purpose of my journey?

The Indian government, ever since Ananda Marga had grown so large and international, did not issue visas to anyone they knew was an Ananda Margii. Most overseas workers took care to appear like general tourists when visiting Baba, although occasionally someone became blacklisted. I knew that officials on the Bangladesh-Indian border were less likely to ask any questions.

From Dhaka, I had to travel by bus, then take a ferry boat and a rickshaw to the border. At the border town, just before crossing, I met two overseas didis on their way for the same avadhutika initiation. They had an even harder journey than I did. Most people cannot imagine young Western women undergoing such measures to meet their guru for an initiation. But disciples often endured amazing trials for such a special occasion. Generally, when one underwent such difficulties, the disciple felt a sense of protection. I felt Baba's presence on my solo journey across Bangladesh.

When all the candidates had gathered in Kolkata, our supervisors advised us to not visit Baba's quarters. Instead, we should remain in the didis' headquarters and practice speaking Bengali. They said, "Baba is in a testy mood. He has asked if you are versed in Bengali, as every acharya studied it when they completed acharya training. Better you study here until Baba calls you for *diiksa* (initiation) so no one can test your skills in Bengali."

The reason Baba may have been so particular about Bengali at this time was He had begun dictating during Sunday darshans a demi-encyclopedia on the Bengali alphabet. He would introduce a letter, use examples of common Bengali words that started with that letter, and explain how these words were derived and changed over time. Baba also weaved interesting, funny, and spiritual stories during the explanations.

While Baba dictated His demi-encyclopedia on the Bengali language, He introduced ten new letters to be added to the Bengali alphabet in order to improve its versatility. Years later His demi-encyclopedia would be recognized by many noted linguistic Indian and Bangladesh scholars to be used in their universities.

With Baba so focused on Bengali, we didis grouped together and studied basic Bengali every day at the Tiljala headquarters. During the day we met in Auntie's room and studied together while she watched and advised us. During one such session, she stopped our Bengali drilling and took us in another direction.

"What is the meaning of devotion? Can you define it for me?" asked Auntie.

I answered her using the theme from a Baba quote, "It makes the mind so soft and tender while keeping it durable and strong."

Auntie answered, "Is that so? Is that what devotion is?"

Others told their definitions of love. But each time Auntie would respond as if she was remembering something much more. "I don't know; is that so? What is devotion?"

We began to understand that this was similar to a Zen koan and no answer would do. It was like the Zen koan, "What is the sound of one hand clapping?"

The mystery of divine love had to be experienced and words were inadequate. Her inquiries filled the room with love and wonder. With Auntie's inspiration and the camaraderie of studying together, we spent two days pleasantly studying while we waited for diiks'a.

One afternoon we were called to Baba's quarters for diiks'a. We were told that Baba might give it in Bengali. Hearing this gave me concern as I thought it might deter my initiation since I was not fluent in Bengali. I wondered, "Am I really worthy of such an opportunity?"

We went upstairs and waited excitedly outside of Baba's room. Inside His room, Baba was angrily shouting in Bengali, and we learned that He had just removed Didi Ananda Karuna's avadhutikaship. She was being reprimanded due to us candidates but I did not hear the details. He was holding her responsible for us in some way. Often Baba gave the seniors punishments for their juniors' mistakes. In this way, Baba emphasized our responsibility as leaders.

All this occurred minutes before we entered His room. When it came time and we were called into Baba's room, we did not know what to expect. But Baba immediately lightened our spirits by saying, "I thought to speak to you in Bengali, but for your convenience, I will converse in English."

After our time with Baba, we returned to the didis' quarters and met with Auntie to learn more individually with her. At midnight we began to practice the new meditation we had learned. This was to be done every month on the new moon night. The next morning we awoke early and dressed in new orange saris to signify our greater commitment. Then we left for the market to purchase garlands for Baba and sweets for our seniors. I bought a beautiful white jasmine garland for Baba.

Upon reaching Baba's quarters, each of us received a new avadhutika name. My new name was "Ananda Nivedita." At this point, celebrating generally began. But because of Didi Ananda Karuna's situation, we could not rejoice. The festive mood had to be suppressed until her situation was normalized. Right before Baba went on His field walk, He lifted her punishment and freed us to begin our celebrations. We felt grateful to Didi Ananda Karuna for facing difficulty on our behalf and for helping us.

After His morning field walk Baba stopped to talk to the new avadhutikas. I stepped up to Him and offered my flower garland. As I offered it He asked, "And what is your new name?"

"I'm Ananda Nivedita," I replied.

I placed the fragrant garland around His neck. Promptly He told me the meaning of my name, "She who offers herself at the altar of the Supreme."

The synchronicity of the offering of the garland over his head while he told me the meaning of my name, which matched my own heart's wish, made this moment the zenith point of my life. He was my altar of the Supreme and He knew I felt this way. After a brief pause, Baba turned from me and talked to other new avadhutikas. Then He went inside the house. I was a happy daughter of the Supreme Father.

23
In Malaysia

When I returned to my sector, my supervisor asked me to turn over my work in Jakarta to another didi and to proceed to Malaysia. I was to build a base for the didis in Kuala Lumpur, the capital city of Malaysia. Immediately upon arriving in Kuala Lumpur, I searched for a house suitable for a new preschool and living quarters. The dadas already had a meditation center close to Kuala Lumpur. I decided to choose Kajang, a town in the eastern part of Malaysia located twenty-one kilometers from Kuala Lumpur. I rented a house and began a preschool and yoga classes there.

The history of Malaysia is interesting and diverse. Because it was located on an important sea-lane, from its start it was opened to global trade and foreign cultural influence, especially from India and China from the seventh to the fourteenth centuries. Later, with the increase of Islamic traders in the fourteenth and fifteenth centuries, Islam was established and sultanates arose. During the period of European imperialism, the Portuguese established themselves on the Malay Peninsula in 1511, followed by the Dutch in 1641. The British gained full domination over the entire Peninsula in 1824, only to quit after World War II. At this time Malaysia went through a period of nationalism and insurgency until it gained independence in 1957.

Malaysia has a multi-ethnic and multi-cultural population consisting of Malays, Chinese, and Indians. There is racial tension between these group, especially the Malays and Chinese. In the 1960s, racial strife culminated with Singapore's separation from Malaysia in 1965 and the imposition of emergency rule in Malaysia in 1969. Until this day, emergency rule has not fully been reversed.

Despite undertows of unrest, Malaysia's growing prosperity lessened some of the political discontent. I liked living in Malaysia with its prosperity and rich, diverse cultures. To my surprise, the yoga classes I started in Kajang became very popular and grew in size. The preschool, however, remained small with eight children whom I taught myself. Due to the popularity of the yoga classes, another didi came and joined me to help keep them growing.

Every weekend I would spend Friday night in Seremban, a neighboring city, and Saturday and Sunday in Melaka. By establishing routine visits, it helped to strengthen the local Margiis and aided the forming of local units there.

One major benefit of living in Malaysia was that I could easily visit Baba in India. Whenever my supervisory didi could not attend senior RDS in Kolkata, I would act as her representative. One of these occasions coincided with a celebration to mark Baba's completion of 3,200 Prabhat Samgiita songs. On this occasion about a hundred Kolkata Margiis, dadas, and didis gathered at the darshan hall in Baba's Lake Garden's house. The hall was full and yet its small size lent a cozy atmosphere to the occasion. Various Prabhat Samgiitas were sung for Baba. The highlight of the evening was a dance performance of Prabhat Samgiita by an older girl from the didis' Tiljala girls home. After her performance, Baba complimented the young girl's artistry.

The sweet mood generated at this celebration carried on throughout RDS. Our meetings with Baba were full of serenading and there was light encouragement rather than punishment. Due to His sweetness, it was difficult to leave.

On the morning of my departure, I purchased a white jasmine garland to offer Baba. To my delight, on His return from His field walk He accepted it and let me place the garland around His head. I treasured this rare privilege and wrote a poem about it:

The Garlanding

A girl kept her jasmine garland bundled in palm leaves
To hide its perfume from the air's wafts.
She smiled at the thought of her guru's pleasure
How He would savor the bouquet.
Her young mind, a tiny bird hopping on a limb of life,
Watched for any signs of His arrival.
Anticipation became rocks to cross time's river.
Suddenly electricity filled the air, announcing His arrival.
Her heart drummed welcome, as she garlanded Him with
her love's lea.

After RDS with Baba, I returned to Kajang and resumed my busy routine. A couple of months later I received a call from my supervisor asking me to fly back to Kolkata and replace her again for senior RDS. Surprised by this sudden, repeated good fortune, I began my preparations to leave.

The highlight of this particular visit occurred on the Sunday-evening darshan with the Kolkata Margiis. Many people were in attendance so the hall was packed. We were so squeezed together on the floor it was hard to find a place for our knees unless we sat like a ball, all tucked in, rather than cross-legged. Throughout the evening Baba spoke mostly in Bengali. One Indian didi who sat next to me translated some of His talk for me and for others from overseas.

During the darshan Baba explained to the Margiis what it was like to be a genius. He explained that usually a person was born a genius. On rare occasions by divine grace, an individual can rise to this level. At that point, Baba asked for a volunteer for a demonstration. A young man in the audience who was an active Margii in the Kolkata region stood up. Baba pointed at him with His cane and informed, "I am temporarily giving this boy the ability to experience what a genius would perceive. Tell us what do you see?" said Baba.

The young man answered, "I am thinking of my mother and her image is as clear as if she were standing in front of me."

Baba explained that this man was briefly experiencing what it was like to be a genius. Then He said, "With more meditation and through grace, you can all achieve such ability."

This experience encouraged me greatly. I believed with more effort and love, I could achieve greater mental ability. I went back to my field invigorated and inspired.

Kajang Malaysian Preschool

24
Return to Manila

In the late 1980s, Baba supervised all of Ananda Marga's organizational growth, the garden program, created Prabhat Samgiita music, dictated the demi-encylcopedia of Bengali, and then gave another new theory. In 1987 He propounded the theory of microvita. Microvita, according to Baba, are "the mysterious emanation of the cosmic factor."

Physical microvita are subtle and smaller than atoms, electrons, or protons. These physical microvita have little to do with carbon atoms, yet are fundamental to all living beings' existence. In the psychic sphere, subtle psychic microvita exist that are more subtle than ectoplasm. Baba gave thirty-eight discourses on this topic that were published. He told us to start microvita research right away as it would greatly benefit society.

In an effort to keep up with Baba's new philosophical theories and His organizational targets, I was very busy with my private and social development. This was a very happy time of life for me and I felt light inside. One day I received an unexpected call from my head didi, telling me to leave the work I was doing in Kajang to the didi who had been assisting me and fly directly to Manila. I was getting a new assignment to act as the Women's Welfare Department office secretary, in addition to my ongoing HPMGL work. I immediately relinquished my work to the other didi and flew to Manila.

While I had been in Malaysia, a dynamic co-worker named Didi Ananda Mitra had arranged the purchase of a house in Manduluyong, Philippines, which lay on the outskirts of Manila city. This was to become the new didis' sectorial office. During my time I stayed there, at least six people lived at our sectorial office and often more.

My head didi arranged for six little girls to be moved from our other children's homes to live with us. It was our practice to have children live with us at our office and residence where possible. We would become a family to one another. The children's home girls came originally from various slums. Their parents had relinquished their full custody to Ananda Marga due to various reasons, particularly financial ones. They were too poor to care for these girls. When we did relief work in the slums where they lived, we met these parents. By regularly meeting them during social service, they grew to trust us and to believe we could offer their children a better life. So along with my new office duties, the local diocese secretary didi and I shared responsibility and care for these six little girls.

My prior experience with children's homes was as a visitor. This was my first experience of full responsibility for raising the children. The girls were aged three to ten years old and they struggled to adjust to a new lifestyle. They had to do regular meditation and eat a vegetarian diet, which was new to them. We had to step up to fulfill their physical and emotional needs. It took us a good year to understand one another better.

During my second year with the children, we grew to love and appreciate one another. It surprised me how eager I became to find ways to improve their lives and their happiness. While out for the day, I looked forward to returning home and to being with the children. I found that life details like their school, health, food, clothes, and recreation became important. Sometimes I had to stay up late and nurse a sick child, and I found my heart wrenched while she suffered. Often the girls accompanied me to various events, and I discovered many ways to make them happier. The other women who visited or stayed at the didi's sectorial office also contributed to the girls' well-being. I remember this period of my life as homey and pleasant.

While I focused on office work and the children, with the help of another Margii sister, I started a kindergarten in Isla Puting Batu, the large slum near the port. Two of our girls came from there. This slum was the one I had regularly visited with Dada Adveshananda ten years earlier as a new didi in Manila Sector. Now, with the formation of the kindergarten there, I could measure my growth over the past ten years.

Around this time I had a splendid Baba dream. Throughout my Marga life, I have been blessed occasionally with dreams of Him. In this dream I was at Ananda Nagar and witnessed that Baba had left His quarters and was walking alone with a towel around His neck, preparing to go into a nearby bathhouse. In deference for His privacy, I maintained my distance and watched Him go into the bathhouse. Soon afterward, He left it and returned to His house. I slipped inside the bathhouse to experience the room that Baba had just vacated. I saw that on its cement floor a miracle had occurred. Where Baba had stood, His feet had etched footprints into the cement. A wave of longing for Him came over me. I wanted to lie down and roll my body on His footprints and cover myself with His vibration. As soon as I lay down, I awoke from my dream and felt a surge of energy rising up my spine. A voice in my head said, "Lord of the Universe."

The euphoria from that Baba dream lasted a long time and the beauty of the imagery is unforgettable.

Living in Manila at the women's office meant being in the hub of our sector's dealings. Regularly there was reporting and functions to attend. It felt exciting to be well-informed about the latest information on Baba and our sector's progress. In this way, three years passed quickly. But I began to miss meeting Baba so I asked for an opportunity to attend DMC at Ananda Nagar.

When I went, I expected this visit to India to be similar to my previous visits. It was initially. For two weeks I enjoyed a blissful and inspiring visit. Then toward the end of the function, new postings were announced and I was surprised to learn I had been transferred to Suva Sector in a newly created post called "Sectorial Girls' Prout."

To be transferred to a new continent and assignment floored me. My supervisor and I had a congenial relationship and she shared most things with me. I had no inkling of this transfer. After I learned about it, she took me aside and explained that she had been asked to put forward the name of a capable didi to take on the role of Sectorial Girl's Prout (GP). When she put up my name for this position in Manila Sector, an unexpected twist occurred. There was a need to transfer a didi who worked in Girl's Prout in Suva Sector. Central leaders told my head didi that because I had lived many years in Manila Sector, it was ideal to interchange the Suva didi with me. Quickly, it came to pass and my supervisor could not stop it.

The news stunned me. After leaving Ananda Nagar and arriving in our central office in Kolkata, I was asked to immediately move to the Girl's Prout central office. Since Girl's Prout is a different organization than Ananda Marga, it has its own headquarters and activities. Baba set up Ananda Marga to do His spiritual work and PROUT to implement His economic and political vision. These would run independently of each other. The land for the GP office had been purchased and built a few years after the central office was constructed. It was located across the street from the women's central office.

The GP didis were very nice and welcoming to me but my heart felt heavy. I really felt bereft leaving the Ananda Marga headquarters where my friends were. I was worried about facing the children with the news of my transfer. After a few days, I flew back to Manila to collect my possessions and turn over my work to another didi. I said a tearful goodbye to the children and other people. It was sad, especially for the children who did not fully understand why I had to leave them. After this experience, I did not want to work in a children's home again because the inevitable posting transfer was too hard. Even knowing they would be well cared for and loved by other didis did not make it any better. I dutifully did what was bidden and left Manila Sector for Suva Sector.

Children's Home the Day I Left for Suva Sector

25
Australian Life

MOST PEOPLE I met in Australia welcomed me warmly, but inwardly I missed the children. For the first time, I understood heartbreak. It took three years to heal the ache caused by leaving the home children. I also missed the Asian culture that I had worked so hard to adopt. There were also additional factors that slowed my adjustment.

My assignment in GP was so different from any previous ones. My new supervisory didi explained that now I had to work mostly with women who wanted to advocate for social change in the political arena. I was to maintain a separation from the women involved with Ananda Marga.

This left me to function more independently than I previously experienced. The trouble with this arrangement, I realized, was I enjoyed being closely connected to other workers and active Margiis. I appreciated having a supervisor to conspire with more than my freedom. Also, my previous experience lay in the field of education and not politics. I felt out of my depth in my new position.

PROUT is very important and I knew it was a vital part of Baba's heritage to the world. In His social, economic, and political philosophy, He clarified why communism and capitalism were faulty theories that could not uplift society. Instead, PROUT offered sustainable guidelines for society's progress. But most political change is difficult to enact, as those in power do not want to relinquish it. Plus PROUT implementation, in particular, requires exemplary moral leadership, and such leaders have not surfaced.

Too many dynamic people are either overburdened with their personal survival or seduced by materialistic trends.

In many ways, PROUT work should have been a good fit for me. I deeply loved its tenets and I understood the dynamism and unpredictability of politics. While working in Manila Sector I had witnessed the suffering under the dictator, Ferdinand Marcos. In 1986 I experienced the exhilaration of the People Power Revolution that toppled him. When I visited Suva in 1987 I witnessed men walking in the streets with guns, the ousting of the newly elected people's representative, the proclaiming of Fiji as a Republic, and the end of its participation in the British Commonwealth. These experiences showed me how organic and changeable are governments. Throughout my travels, I observed various systems of government and their difficulties and understood the need for PROUT in the world.

Upon beginning my PROUT work in Australia, I realized that my new post afforded me an opportunity to work with many dynamic individuals. The women I collaborated with were established activists in various fields like Aboriginal rights, anti-uranium mining protests, and pro-gay rights. They were sharp-witted Proutists who could astutely argue an array of political and social issues in the light of PROUT tenets. Because they were so dynamic, I co-functioned with them instead of being the initiator as I had done in Manila Sector. Together we published a magazine every other month and did other social work. Most of the women I worked with lived in Sydney so my base was there. Occasionally I toured Brisbane, Melbourne, and Lismore as well.

While acclimating to my new assignment, I went through various cultural clashes after living so long in Southeast Asia. The standard of living in Australia contrasted greatly with the Philippines and Indonesia. As one of the wealthier countries, Australia seemed a land of opportunity. But it was also very materialistic. My new role in PROUT caused me to become aware of the Aboriginals and their treatment. They seemed worse off than their Asian counterparts. What remained of the Aboriginal culture primarily was found in the isolated areas of the outback. The outback lies at the center of Australia and is its largest portion of land. But the outback is the flattest, oldest, and least fertile soil on the earth. Most Australians live near the coasts where the tropical rainforests and resources are.

A year had passed since my transfer and I was still experiencing inner grief when suddenly I was transferred again. Baba had ordered every non-Indian didi who held the post of Sectorial Girl's Prout throughout the world to be immediately transferred to another post. Baba said to central workers that only didis originating from India should hold the sectorial GP post. At this juncture of Ananda Marga, it appeared Baba wanted mostly Indian workers in the highest posts. My new assignment was Guam diocese secretary.

Although many of my colleagues felt unhappy at the preference of Indian workers for the highest posts, I did not mind at this moment. I do not know about those who held the GP assignment in other areas but I believed Baba knew I was unhappy and was responding to it. I also interpreted Baba's directive that increased the number of Indian workers in the upper echelon as a decision by Him to prioritize the propagation of Eastern spiritual culture. During this period Baba was highlighting Bengali with His weekly creation of a Bengali demi-encyclopedia and His daily stream of new Prabhat Samgiitas. I knew that Baba could change this trend at a future juncture.

With the Didis in Suva Sector
(I am in the middle)

26
Guam Posting

*M*Y NEW POST of ladies diocese secretary of Guam meant moving to a small island in Micronesia. After a decade of work, I was no longer a sectorial level worker. The new assignment in Guam, I was told, was a difficult post, as the previous didis had not succeeded in building any base. It was remote to other Ananda Marga hubs. On hearing this, I regretted being transferred there.

At first, some sectorial workers said they would appeal on my behalf in central office for a different location that was in or nearer to Australia. But before this effort could gain any momentum, Baba began to ask my supervisors, "Has Ananda Nivedita reached Guam yet? She should reach immediately."

This was a clear indication it was His urgent and personal decision for me to work there. That meant I not only had to work in Guam but should reach it as soon as possible. No one could intercede in this matter. The only silver lining I felt in learning of this was that Baba wanted me there. It must be the right post for me, I thought.

Guam is the largest and southernmost of the Mariana Islands, centered between Japan, Hawaii, New Guinea, and the Philippines in the Circle of Fire, a volcanic zone. The island is forty-eight kilometers long and six to nineteen kilometers wide in different areas and is entirely surrounded by beautiful coral reefs with deep water channels. Sandy beaches, rocky cliffs, and mangroves characterize the coastline area. Sheer limestone cliffs dominate the north, while the southern end of the island is mountainous.

The indigenous people are the Chamorros, who first inhabited it nearly four thousand years ago. They still are the majority and are often employed as civil servants. In the 1500s Guam became a Spanish colony until it was ceded to the United States after the Spanish-American War. During WWII, between 1941 to 1944, Guam fell under Japanese rule. Later it was regained by the Americans and remains until the present as its territory. The United States presently keeps 42 percent of Guam's land for military bases. The Chamorro, Spanish, Japanese, and American influences are all discernible in Guam's present culture.

Prior to my assignment on Guam, Dada Manovendrananda had begun his work there as a new dada. He had given many meditation classes and had a list of women who wanted to learn meditation. My main difficulty was, "Where do I live and how to support myself?"

I lived initially with a Margii named Vina and her husband, Ed. Workers usually only visit family homes for short stays. But due to the circumstances, they accommodated me for several months. Vina even temporarily employed me in her advertising agency so I could have a source of income. We became fast friends during this stay.

One day Dada Manovendrananda showed me a house that he had learned was available for rent and might be good for a school. We went and inspected it. I agreed that it could be adapted to make a preschool suitable for forty children. He entered into negotiations on my behalf with the owner while I began the various licensing steps to turn the house into a legal preschool. With a loan, I was able to open an Ananda Marga preschool in Dededo.

During the initial years, every dollar I could manage went to the expansion and improvement of this school. In the evenings I attended classes at Guam Community College to fulfill the legal requirements to be the licensed director of the preschool. This brought me into contact with some excellent acquaintances and put me on friendly terms with the college faculty. In fact, I developed such a good relationship with the head of the Early Childhood Education Department, I was invited to be on their advisory committee over the next five years. The college also encouraged their students to visit the Ananda Marga preschool and observe it. Similarly, I made good ties with the local university. I even expanded my social networking and joined and held offices in GAEYC (Guam Early Childhood Education Association) and the Daycare Association of Guam.

Rather quickly the school grew to its full licensed population. I was very engrossed with its management and my networking obligations. Besides my preschool work, I kept up with traditional Ananda Marga work, such as weekly group meditation and yoga classes. Soon I became so busy my supervisor didi sent from Australia a local full-time volunteer named Ketana to help with the Guam work. Ketana was talented in education and helped the school flourish. While she worked there we collaborated on three education teaching books: *I Can Draw the Sun, Safe and Sound,* and *Who Am I?*.

Because of Guam's distance from other Ananda Marga areas, I met other didis only at the annual sectorial retreat in Australia or when I attended DMS in India. Whenever I attended, I enjoyed being with other didis and catching up on their lives and on any organizational changes. When I visited, I habitually I sought out workers and key Margiis focused on education to exchange ideas. There were a good number of people interested in education and in Australia there were several Ananda Marga schools. The creation and maintenance of schools, particularly preschools and kindergartens, was a key direction of our mission since its early years.

Every couple of years, I also visited Baba in India. Because I was no longer a sectorial level worker I did not have much reporting to do. There were fewer meetings to attend. My visits to India were now for inspiration and social fulfillment. To fill the gap that opened from less reporting time, I became more engrossed in our education system while in India. I sought out Ananda Marga educators and exchanged views on how to improve our schools. I took on the assignment of compiling Baba's talks on education for a central office publication called *Discourses on Neo-humanist Education.*

Whenever I saw Baba, I felt more endeared to Him. I am not sure why He seemed more charming and captivating now that I had fewer designated opportunities to meet with Him. I loved going to His quarters to sing Prabhat Samgiita with the crowds every time Baba left and returned from field walk. The crowds had grown in size due to the organization's global expansion and I would stand together with many others in order to catch a glimpse of Him.

The best occasion to visit Baba was January DMC at Ananda Nagar. Then our master unit became an exciting city enhanced by a myriad of tents. In India, they constructed a large tent that accommodated twenty thousand people. Smaller tents clustered nearby selling goods and food.

During DMC, Baba's darshan routinely occurred at noon and night time. In between darshans, I attended various meetings and visited Baba's quarters to serenade Him with Prabhat Samgiita. DMC was also an opportunity to meet with many people from various parts of India and abroad.

The two most important events to attend were Baba's Renaissance Universal talk on the eve of DMC and his DMC evening discourse. Each day Margii artists decorated the pandal where Baba sat. They added new decorations every day to it until the decorations became a stunning visual display on DMC night. Often the decorations incorporated a theme that related to Baba's philosophy.

Among the various Renaissance Universal talks, I was privileged to hear Baba's discourse where he introduced the coming of a pole shift and the advancing of an ice age. It was most vivid for me. I listened in awe as Baba told that the earth was on the precipice of cataclysmic events. In fact, He said, these events were overdue. He did not reassure in His talk that the pole shift and ice age would be beneficial to life as we know it. Thus I and many others walked away after it in a daze.

The next day DMC was very special. The evening started with Baba receiving a garland from the Ananda Nagar rector master. Then He blessed, one by one, recently married Margii couples. The new couples would offer a garland to Baba and He would hold their hands and their garland while He recited "Be like Shiva and Parvati." Then Baba would hand back the garland to the wife as a keepsake. Immediately following their blessings, Baba would bestow awards to a handful of workers and Margiis for their outstanding service in the recent months, such as the best school, best children's home, best diocese, best region, best sector, and the winners of the kaoshikii and tandava competitions. After the awards, beautiful Prabhat Samgiita was sung by all. The songs were led by accomplished singers and musicians and then immediately repeated by the audience. Only after the audience's mood sweetened from singing His music did Baba begin His talk.

Baba seamlessly spoke a mixture of Bengali, Hindi, and English throughout His address which was later translated and published. There were devotional moments when the audience felt so moved by His words that they cried loudly, "Baba, Baba." At the end of His talk, Baba began to recite in various languages a Sanskrit shloka that started, "Let everyone by happy. Let everyone be disease free."

Following the shloka, Baba gave the vharabhaya mudra. He held it for some seconds to allow a wave of energy to pass over the crowd. Responding to the exciting acceleration of energy, people wept, cried out His name, and meditated. Many went into various stages of ecstasy. To unify the moment, the accomplished singers began to lead everyone in Prabhat Samgiita and *avarta* kiirtan, kiirtan in all directions. This was the cue for Baba to depart. When kiirtan began, Baba exited the pandal while He held His hands in Namaskar pose and listened to His devotees sing.

All His darshans these days, every gesture and expression, was beautiful, meaningful, and transported me to some wondrous state. I felt drunk with the joy of Baba's presence and my heart beat with the desire to please Him. Seeing and being with Baba reached new depths.

After DMC it was time to go home or to the central office. The difficult part of visiting Baba at this stage was that the organization had gained complexity, especially when it came to tour program (TP) signing. If I or any worker left the central office, we had to make a TP stating where we will work for the next couple of months. Our TP had to be approved and signed by various supervisors. Although this system was always in effect during my worker life, with the booming organization the number of signatures needed for my TP had increased. There were many didi and dada supervisors to face and some of these could be demanding and troublesome. I loved the organization but during my time as a diocese secretary in Guam its bureaucracy could at times seem like the thorns and Baba the rose.

Annual Picture of Guam Preschool

Office of the President

John T. Cruz
President

OCT 20 1995

Ms. Didi Ananda Nivedita, Director
Ananda Marga Preschool
125 Angela Ct.
Dededo, GU 96912

Dear Ms. Nivedita:

Guam Community College is pleased to inform you of your appointment to the College's Early Childhood Education Advisory Committee. We wish to thank you for your willingness to share your valuable time with us. Your assistance will ensure that high quality occupational education is available to our students and community.

The ultimate objective of the Early Childhood Education Advisory Committee is to maintain and improve educational opportunities for all members of the community who can benefit from the program. Your active attendance, participation and interest in the advisory committee will be influential in helping insure the relevance of our education offerings.

Shortly, you will be notified by College staff about the time, place, date and agenda for the meeting. This meeting will help you better understand the role and function of the committee and your potential contribution to it. You will have an opportunity to meet other members of the committee, College administrators, and the instructional staff.

Thank you again for your interest in Guam Community College's occupational-technical program.

Sincerely,

John T. Cruz
JOHN T. CRUZ

JTC/GSP:vcg
10/19/95

c: Dean, THS
   Early Childhood Education Department

COMMONWEALTH NOW!
P.O. Box 23069, Barrigada, Guam, 96921 • Phone: (671) 734-4311 • Fax: 734-1003

Appointment to Guam College Advisory Board

27
Deep Sorrow

WHILE I LIVED on Guam significant events occurred that impacted me so much they changed my character permanently. During my first year, I learned that Auntie, my beloved elder, had died. I recalled how she repeatedly said, "Baba will not yet sign my tour program."

Finally, Baba had signed her ethereal tour program. Now both Dada Adveshananda and Didi Ananda Bharati had passed. I felt my main mentors were gone and I had to strengthen myself more internally. Despite a tendency to be dependent on supervisors, my years of isolation in Guam from other didis, the responsibility of running a legal school, and the death of my mentors propelled me toward new independence.

Then on October 20, 1990, I received a long distance call from my Guam colleague, Dada Manovendrananda, who was abroad. He said, "I have to tell you something I never imagined would ever occur and that is very difficult to say. Baba has passed away unexpectedly and suddenly from a heart attack. He went to His room to rest after various organizational meetings and died. If you want to see His body and attend His cremation, you have permission to go. You must arrive in Kolkata within the next three days."

Upon hanging up the phone, I told Ketana and Vina this news. Then I retired alone to grieve. In my life, I had never wished to have the power to turn back the clock. Now with all my might I wanted to turn back the time to when Baba was still alive. Overwhelming powerlessness consumed me and my heart felt like it could barely beat under the pressure of the loss. Grief is a vice that squeezes terribly one's heart and tears do not relieve it.

The next day was Sunday and I informed the other Margiis of Baba's death. On Monday I arranged for the management of the school for the next two weeks during Ketana's and my absence. That evening Ketana, Vina, and I flew to Bangkok and the next day we reached Kolkata.

The Tiljala headquarters was in deep sorrow, disbelief, and shock. At times I wondered if Baba might use His occult powers and return from death like someone arising out of a deep coma. Surely He was not leaving us fatherless yet? I thought.

I walked around in a teary state of disbelief, sadness, and loss. The question arose, What will the organization be like without Him physically present to guide us? but I pushed it to the side of my thoughts. I wanted to be fully present with my mind only on Him at His departure.

Baba's body lay inside a glass refrigerated coffin and at any time we were encouraged to walk reverently and quietly around it. We were asked not to touch the coffin or stand by it but rather to quietly walk around it or meditate nearby. On one occasion, central workers asked a group of us to stand around His coffin and take an oath while touching our hearts. This oath came from a meeting Baba had held just days prior to His death. On October 12, 1990, Baba had asked all workers present to pledge while keeping their hands on their hearts: "All my energy, all my mind, all my thoughts, all my deeds are to be goaded into the path of collective elevation of human society, without neglecting other animate and inanimate objects right from this moment until the last point of my living on this earth."

Then Baba asked the workers, "Do you all understand?"

"Yes, Baba!" they answered.

"Can I depend on you?" He asked.

"Yes, Baba!" they again replied.

Now at His coffin side, I took this same oath.

During our grieving, we talked about how we had overlooked the clues that Baba was going to leave His body. We knew He suffered from a severe heart condition that had required hospitalization. His heart and health had been compromised due to His long fast during imprisonment and His vigorous work schedule. In the recent years, Baba had been checked daily by doctors who all urged Him not to work so hard and for such long hours, warning that His body would not endure such strain. But Baba did not heed their advice and did not slow down His routine. Rather He continued, even when He was hospitalized, to create new Prabhat Samgiita songs, conduct various spiritual meetings, and lead organizational meetings.

Right before His death, He had added multiple programs for the master units. A master unit is like an ecovillage and is founded on the principles of sustainable development and self-sufficiency. It is to be a resource for the local area. Currently, there are hundreds of master units around the world, with Ananda Nagar being the most well known and established. Baba had directed Ananda Nagar's development personally through the years, arranged for Ananda Marga's annual global spiritual functions there, and oversaw aid to the neighborhood as it was located in one of the poorest and most backward areas of West Bengal. Ananda Nagar today has various schools with over two thousand students. It has a college, affiliated with Burdwan University, that currently offers bachelor level degrees in the arts and sciences. Besides schools, there is also agriculture, light industry, a charitable hospital, and a children's home.

On September 7, 1990, mere weeks before His death, Baba created Gurukul. Gurukul was important to me ever since Auntie explained it as the system gurus traditionally used to teach their disciples. Baba now used this term to refer to Ananda Marga's global network for propagating educational ideas, curricula, and teacher training. It formalized what He offered His disciples for the wider public through spiritual schools. Throughout His life as the guru of Ananda Marga, He had mostly avoided the public.

Now, through Gurukul, He was going to be a guru for the public with schools that enabled children to learn meditation, morality, and spirituality. Baba's last Prabhat Samgiita, number 5018, was the Gurukul song and its translation is as follows:

> We shall establish Gurukul. We shall color with the effulgence of knowledge each and every bud and flower. No one will lag behind. We shall play each string of our lyre. We shall thread together all with the twine of love. We shall create an incomparable garland of gems. No one will be left aside or looked down upon. All will live as in their own family, their minds filled with affection and sweetness for all.

These last programs brought Baba's earthly sojourn to a conclusion. If we had not been so blind, we might have appreciated His last years as His final bequests. But, despite the clues, most people in Ananda Marga believed that Baba was invincible and would not die soon. Most disciples believed Baba had tacitly agreed to live until 2005 so we disregarded any sign to the contrary. We remembered His trials in jail and His long fasting only as miracles that demonstrated life was at His command with little understanding of how much it had weakened His physical body.

On the day of His cremation, so many devotees gathered that it looked like a sea of life surrounding the pyre. On every rooftop, every available land surface, thousands and thousands of people gathered. Despite the immense multitude of people, the atmosphere was very respectful and dignified.

Baba's body was carried out in the glass coffin by many dadas. Those selected to carry the coffin were senior dadas who had been with Baba for many years. They now had the honor to carry His body to the pyre. Baba's adopted son, Kinshuk, lit the funeral pyre.

At the early onset of the cremation process, some overseas Margiis began to sing Baba Nam Kevalam. Initially, this caused a confusion to rumble through the crowd as Baba's cremation had been planned as an austere, silent occasion. Various workers began to gesture for silence. Then a few senior dadas on top of a nearby roof joined the overseas Margiis in singing, signaling their agreement. Baba wanted this loving serenade and tribute so thousands of people joined in to sing Baba Nam Kevalam.

When the pyre was lit and the flames rose higher, fed by ghee and wood, a deep hush fell over the crowd. Overhead a flock of gray doves with one white dove in their midst flew over the pyre, encircled the flames, and flew off toward the clouds. The birds came to pay tribute and escort His spirit onward. The clouds themselves formed into big circular mandalas in the sky and hosted many ethereal beings drawn to the auspicious occasion.

For hours the pyre burnt and for hours Ketana, Vina, and I sat together with many others to keep a loving vigil in silence. When night came, while the corpse burnt, I could see the sparks fly toward us from the pyre blown by the wind. Ashes frequently landed on our heads and filled our breaths. While inhaling His ashes, I felt Baba's last physical essence went inside me.

Throughout the cremation, my sorrow was mixed with an effort to send goodwill and love with Him on His onward journey. Baba had made it clear that He would keep taking birth on different planets to uplift the universe. I hope to be with Him again, I thought.

The next day there were small meetings and we were informed that the highest governing board of purodhas would soon convene to determine the next president of Ananda Marga. Baba would remain our guru guiding us from other realms. But we needed a new organizational leader. I had an idea whom the purodhas would select but could not wait for those proceedings. There was the school demanding our return so we had to fly back.

Later I learned on October 31 that Acharya Shraddhananda Avadhuta became the purodha pramukha and president of Ananda Marga. He was the first in succession after Baba's departure.

Back on Guam, I faced disturbing feelings and thoughts, as I had waited to return from India before reflecting on them. At times I felt that a wrenching primal sadness and loss would consume me if I thought about life without Baba's colorful presence and guidance. Vivid memories of being with Him kept flashing in my brain. On the practical side, I wondered what would the organization be like without Baba directing every important detail? It was the end of Baba giving new ideas, new programs, and darshans to charm and uplift. I now would have to trust that Baba directed the organization through others.

I also needed to come to terms with Baba's leaving in regards to my meditation. Whenever I sat for meditation, Baba seemed alive and available. It was confusing to miss Him so much and then be consoled by His presence in meditation. Was I giving Him proper respect by being so sad about His physical departure when He was still alive in my meditation? These conflicting ideas plagued me. I reflected how Baba had prepared me for this time by posting me to Guam. I had become habituated to turning inward for Him rather than outward. For the first time, I was glad that I was in Guam where I could be alone with my thoughts and feelings.

The school kept running at full attendance and I was busy with it. After school, I held yoga classes, group meditations, and networking. Keeping busy I knew was good therapy for sorrow. A year went by and Ketana returned to Australia, leaving me even busier. Soon I had an opportunity to purchase the school building that we had been renting. After its purchase, I began a huge renovation project, acting as a general contractor and hiring plumbers, masons, and electricians. We added two bathrooms, reroofed the lanai, retiled the floor, added a private kitchenette, and installed energy efficient windows. Most of the improvements got accomplished on the weekends but some were accomplished when the preschool was forced to close for several weeks following a super typhoon and a major earthquake.

Watching the school blossom and transform both physically and psychologically moved me to write about education and psychology. This resulted in the published books *Teach Me to Fly* and *Head in the Stars, Feet on the Ground*.

Running the school on my own, renovating, writing, networking, and other Ananda Marga activities began to exhaust me. I ignored the tiredness and kept going. Most of the time I felt weary and suspected that my body was growing ill from overexertion. Finally, at one sectorial RDS, I told my supervisor that my health was deteriorating. I reminded her that I had been isolated from other didis for a decade.

Over the years I had occasionally asked for reposting due to Guam's isolation from other workers, especially other didis. But each time my supervisor had responded, "There is no one qualified at this time to take your place."

That was why I was surprised when a posting change occurred soon after my talking with my head didi. I was further amazed that the didi who was coming to replace me arrived within a few months of the announcement.

My last large work on Guam occurred as I prepared for my departure. I was invited to serve as the representative for private daycares and preschools on the Governor's Special Task Force. The task force's goal was to create a concrete vision for Guam's early childhood education. The governor hoped it would help Guam's children better enter the new millennium. I was one of a team of thirty people representing military, private, and government arenas that served young children. My specific contribution was to draft new preschool/daycare standards. Before I left Guam, I accomplished this job and submitted it to the task force. I later learned little concrete results came from the task force's efforts other than the creation of a hopeful vision for its children's future.

28
Taipei Life

In 1999 I flew to my new post as Hong Kong Sector's WWD office secretary and diocese secretary of Taipei. Taipei City is the seat of the central government of Taiwan. Officially Taiwan is known as the Republic of China and was formed in 1945. Today, although there are disputes regarding its sovereignty with mainland China, Taiwan continues to establish itself as a republic. Throughout the past century, it has had much growth, ranking it as advanced in terms of freedom of the press, health care, public education, economic freedom, and human development.

My intention in my new assignment was to slow down and regain my health. Unfortunately, I could not slow down. The Chinese Margiis were industrious, disciplined, and self-motivated people who offered dadas and didis many opportunities to participate. Ananda Marga in Taipei had numerous meditation groups and hundreds of Margiis. I was very busy with Margii activities.

Both the dadas' and didis' sectorial offices were located in Taipei so they were hubs, beehives of activity. I loved being there and found it very uplifting. It was a happy time for me aside from my health. In that regard, my health worsened and my body became more painful. Usually, I ignored this and kept up a fast pace of life.

Due to my experience with schools, I focused on improving the preschool there. I arranged with my head didi to permit the building that the didis owned to be converted into a preschool. In return, the preschool paid rent to the didis that enabled them to rent a better office. This gave us a better and more stable site for the children.

While I worked in Taipei, there were rumors of disturbing changes occurring in Ananda Marga at the central office. Among the dadas and didis there had been a unified consensus after Baba's death to respect His passing by maintaining things as they were for twelve years. Differences of opinion among seniors workers had been put aside and workers practiced patience. At the end of twelve years, diverse outlooks grew pronounced and competed with each other. A split was occurring in the organization.

This disharmony was disconcerting to everyone. But with my health deteriorating, I did not have the energy to take sides or contemplate it deeply. My supervisor was concerned about my health and told me to see a doctor. The doctor did some tests but could not determine what was wrong. The Margiis brought me to a Chinese doctor for a consultation. He said, "You will expire soon and Western doctors will wonder what caused it. You need herbs and rest."

This validated how I felt, but aside from beginning a regimen of Chinese herbs, there was little else to be done. At this time I was suddenly promoted to sectorial Progressive Women's Spiritual Association (PWSA). My supervisor told me to turn over my Taipei work to another didi and go to Japan to aid a school in Fukuoka and to meet the PWSA didi living in Kyoto whom I would be replacing. When I received my new orders my only concern was whether my health was up to it. I suppressed my doubts and began preparations to leave.

One day while sitting in the sectorial office I went on the Internet to distract myself from not feeling well. I found myself thinking of a childhood girlfriend so I logged onto a school website. To my surprise a few days later I received an email from an old boyfriend from my youth. He was curious about my life. I responded telling him about Ananda Marga and my missionary life. This reminded me how small and connected was our world.

台北市私立阿南達國際語文學校畢業生合影 90年7月

Annual Picture of Taipei Preschool

29
Japan Days and the Return to the USA

*A*FTER TURNING OVER my work to my replacement, I flew to Japan and began my orientation to its environment and culture. Japan is an island country, consisting of thousands of islands. It has a large economy and is affluent. What made Japan special for me was the concern they showed for their environment and culture. Even a tiny plot of land in front of a house would have a beautiful oriental garden, and they were proud of their traditions.

I flew into Osaka International Airport and was greeted by the didi I was replacing and some local Margiis. They drove me to Kyoto where the didi rented a two-story house for her school and residence. The city of Kyoto was arranged in traditional Chinese Feng Shui style with the Imperial Palace, an important landmark, facing south. The east sector of the capital lay to the west, and the west sector sat to the east. The northern area, being less populated, remained more quaint and green. Didi's house was located in the northern area.

Didi was a gracious host and explained to me about her PWSA work in the sector and in Japan. After staying with her for three weeks, I left for our school in Fukuoka to temporarily supervise it. It was located in a traditional Japanese house with floors covered in thick tatami mats and had a small beautiful garden. The school had an enrollment of fourteen children. Due to my previous education experience of running schools, I saw ways to improve its schedule, curriculum, and layout. The two Japanese women who were employed as teachers welcomed these suggestions.

Field Trip with Fukuoka Preschool

I liked living in Fukuoka, which is the capital city of Fukuoka Prefecture and lies on the northern shore of the island of Kyushu. Different than the historically charming Kyoto, Fukuoka was an amazingly well laid-out city with many green spaces. It is ranked as one of the world's most livable cities.

Again I was busy with school work, and I found the parents were delighted with the new improvements. I felt content with the school's progress but there was a growing alarm at my deteriorating health. It had worsened to the point that it was impeding my work. I found it difficult now to even walk across the room to help a student.

While I was in Fukuoka I continued to correspond with the friend from my youth that I had become reacquainted with on the Internet. One day he asked in an email if he could visit Fukuoka and see my work. I agreed that it would be interesting for him. When he arrived, he saw how ill I was. Before he left my friend asked me to stop working and return with him to the States. "Instead of dying," he said, "You should take care of your health and continue to help others in other ways. I will support you."

I thought over what my friend said, as I did not want to become a burden to Ananda Marga and I did not want to die like the Chinese doctor said. After six months of deliberating, I decided to stop decades of missionary work. I felt deep regret for disappointing the mission, but I chose life, the chance to serve in a lesser capacity, and the opportunity to keep meditating and loving Baba.

Without telling anyone my plans, I arranged for another didi to take over the school and quietly left the sector. I married my past friend and was grateful he decided to meditate. Immediately I began to rest and maintain a lighter activity load. The service work I did now focused on the propagation of Ananda Marga in my new area. To accomplish this I organized two weekly meditation groups. Through these groups, I met and meditated with many good people. Several of them went on to learn meditation from visiting acharyas. Many became friends.

Over the next years of a lighter activity load my health slowly improved. The love I received from family and friends verified that Baba's grace was with me and I was part of the universal family. I learned that devotion to Baba will always save one and I kept devotion for Him blazing inside of me. I cherish the memory of my life as His missionary worker and would have liked to serve my entire life as an acharya, but life often unfolds differently than expected. I hope the new life lessons that I learn will help me in my next life to be a better disciple.

Epilog

During the formatting of this book, my husband, Rob Gannon ("Ravi"), passed unexpectedly after suffering four brain hemorrhages. His death irrevocably opened a new chapter in my life. Reviewing in my mind's eye our marriage years, especially the later ones, they were full of happiness. My husband was an empathetic, humorous, and kind partner. Above all he made me feel precious, which was a great gift to give another. His love opened my heart wider to the world in many unexpected ways. I am very grateful to Rob, my "Ravi," and hope his soul finds expansion day by day.

Ravi and Me

Postscript

Given the sacrifice and dedication required to do the work of Ananda Marga, I believe the dadas, didis, and active Margiis who work for Baba's mission are heroes. They are the vanguard of a more just and spiritual world. Anyone who ever served alongside them, no matter where or for how long, is part of the rich soil of the mission. I believe the roots of Baba's teachings are deep and spreading, bringing forth a new age on this Earth.

Now with the completion of this writing, I have honored Baba's request at our first meeting when He revealed His luminous body of light and said, "Has the darshan been translated into English? It should be; it must be; it should be!"

I know now His darshan was a much bigger story of love and light than I anticipated when it initially occurred. His darshan was a gift and it was a great honor to share it with you. Baba Nam Kevalam. Love Is all there is.

Acknowledgements

I had many editors who helped me whenever I struggled with my grammar. They further encouraged me to keep writing when I wondered if it was good enough. Thank you to Ann Huber, Steve Merill, Sea Daniels, Jessica McMains, Linda Usita and Mirra Price for their help in editing. I am especially grateful to Devashish who helped me with formatting and publishing.

About the Author

One night, Nancy Gannon had an inspirational dream of her guru handing out various accomplishments, such as a college education and oratory skill, as presents. She watched her guru give someone a gift she coveted. Then He gave her a gift and she woke up. In time, Nancy realized it was the gift of writing. She was not the usual writer, however. Rather, her drive and inspiration came from the guru. Her earlier publications are *For Universal Minds, Teach Me to Fly* and *Head in the Stars, Feet on the Ground*. She has also collaborated on three educational books: *I Can Draw the Sun, Safe and Sound,* and *Who Am I?*

www.ingramcontent.com/pod-product-compliance
Lightning Source LLC
Chambersburg PA
CBHW021110080526
44587CB00010B/459